Anne in action at Library Solutions Institute and Press, 1994, and at UC Berkeley Library, ca. 1984 (inset). Photographs courtesy Suzanne Calpestri.

Technology In Libraries

Essays in Honor of
Anne Grodzins Lipow

Edited by
Roy Tennant

Lulu.com • 2008

Tennant, Roy.
    Technology in libraries : essays in honor of Anne Grodzins Lipow /
Roy Tennant, editor. — Lulu.com, 2008.
    vii, 110 p. : ill. ; 23 cm.
    Includes bibliographical references and index.
    ISBN 978-0-6152-1212-8

Published by Lulu.com. This book is also available as a free download at
http://techinlibraries.com/ .

Contents

Foreword
Roy Tennant

On September 9, 2004 librarianship lost a true champion. Anne Grodzins Lipow was unique – of all the testimonials I've read about her that is one undeniable truth. We each knew a different set of Anne's qualities, or engaged with her in a different way, but in the end it all came down to the fact that Anne was someone we could all say was "larger than life".

The days after her passing were filled with personal testimonials that were mostly lodged as comments on the Infopeople blog. It was an odd experience for me to read these messages and realize that as much as I felt that I knew her, I barely knew her at all. I was like the proverbial blind man with his hands wrapped around one part of the elephant, while others had a firm grip on other body parts and would describe a very different animal. My reality, as deeply felt as it was, was only a pale shadow of the whole.

But for all that, it was a long, long shadow. As a newly-minted librarian at UC Berkeley in the second half of the 1980s, I knew Anne as the person who led the outreach and instructional efforts of the library. Before long, she saw in me the potential to be a good teacher, despite my fear of public speaking, so she pulled me into her program and began teaching me everything she knew about speaking, putting on workshops, making handouts, etc. Under her tutelage, I taught classes such as dialup access to the library catalog, when 300bps modems were still common.

As the Internet began making inroads into universities, Anne was there with newly developed workshops on how to use it. She was convinced very early on, as was I, that the Internet would be an essential technology for libraries. This led to her approaching my colleague John Ober (then on faculty at the library school at Berkeley) and I about doing a full-day Internet workshop scheduled to coincide with the 1992 ALA Annual Conference in San Francisco. Using a metaphor of John's, we called it "Crossing the Internet Threshold".

In preparing for the workshop, we created so many handouts that we needed to put them into a binder that began to look increasingly like a book in the making. With typical Anne flair, she arranged for the gifted librarian cartoonist Gary Handman (also our colleague at Berkeley) to create a snazzy cover for the binder, that she also used to create T-shirts (which many of us have to this day).

Anne knew enough about workshops to do a "trial run" before the big day, so we did one for UC Berkeley library staff a couple weeks before, which gave us feedback essential to making an excellent workshop. In the end, the workshop was such a hit that Anne ran with it. She took the binder of handouts we had created and made a book out of it — the first book of her newly-created business called Library Solutions Institute and Press. Her decision to publish the book herself rather than seek out a publisher was so typical of Anne. And *how* she did it will tell you a lot about her.

Despite the higher cost, Anne insisted on using domestic union printing shops for printing. While other publishers were publishing books overseas for a fraction of the cost, publishing for Anne was a political and social activity, through which she could do good for those around her. It was very important to her to treat people with respect and kindness, and she did it so well. That was the kind of person Anne was.

While every publisher I have since worked with after Anne has insisted they are incapable of paying royalties any more frequently than twice a year, Anne paid her authors **monthly**. And whereas other publishers wait months to pay you for royalties earned long before, Anne would pay immediately. This meant that when books were returned, as they sometimes were, she took the loss for having paid the author royalties on books that had not been sold. That was the kind of person Anne was.

Anne continued to blaze new trails after libraries began climbing on the Internet bandwagon, due in no small measure to her books and workshops on the topic. Anne became a well-known and coveted consultant on a number of topics, but in particular on reference services. Her "Rethinking Reference" institutes and book were widely acclaimed, and her book *The Virtual Reference Librarian's Handbook* (2003) demonstrated that Anne was always at the cutting edge of librarianship. That was the kind of person Anne was.

I visited her after her cancer was diagnosed and after her treatment had failed. We all knew there was no hope, that she had only a matter of weeks to live. Despite the obvious ravages of the illness, Anne's outlook remained bright and welcoming. She was happy to have her friends and family around her, and we talked of many things except the dark shadow that hung over us all. Even then, she was happy to see whoever came by, and to talk with them with a smile and good wishes. That was the kind of person Anne was.

A piece of all my major professional accomplishments I owe to Anne, and her great and good influence on me. She would deny this, despite it's truth, wanting all the credit to accrue to me alone. That was the kind of person Anne was.

Each one of us who have contributed to this volume have been touched by Anne in our own, quite personal ways. Some of us have known of her work mostly by reputation and reading, while others were blessed with more direct and personal contact. But the fact remains that Anne cast a long professional shadow that will affect many librarians yet to come.

For those of us who created a monument of words to someone we love and respect, Anne had one final gift to give. As anyone who has ever created a present for someone they love knows, in so doing you think about the person for whom you are making the gift. Therefore, the authors of this volume have all spent more time with Anne, and as always it was time well spent. We know our readers will count it so too.

31 January 2008, Sonoma, CA

The Legacy of Anne Lipow
Karen Schneider

Sad News

Anne Lipow, renowned library trainer and consultant, died yesterday, September 9, around 10:30 PM, after a long battle with cancer. Anne was the founder and director of Library Solutions Institute and Press. She was the author of numerous books and articles, including "Crossing the Internet Threshold" and "The Virtual Reference Librarian's Handbook." Her "Rethinking Reference" institutes were recognized as being internationally significant and contributed to Anne's receipt of the ALA Isadore Gilbert Mudge/R.R. Bowker award for "a distinguished contribution to reference librarianship." ...

Posted at 3:52 PM in People | Permalink | Comments (95)

I saw Anne twice in her last few weeks—a time when even knowing she was near death she organized a dinner party for friends, against all advice, to make the house just right, as befit a woman who equipped her kitchen with two ovens so that holiday meals would never feature cold stuffing. But the Anne I remember best was not the Anne of half-tilted hospital beds, trays crowded with prescription pills, or the chalky pallor of late-stage cancer. The Anne I remember best was not even the Anne many of us knew, a bright-eyed sparrow of a librarian who kept her thick brunette hair sensibly bobbed and her pale skin free of makeup and in the tradition of many lifelong Berkeleyans

Karen Schneider is a writer and librarian who has published over 100 articles and 2 books, primarily about Internet technologies for library trade publications. Schneider is also an enthusiastic speaker, presenter, and educator who in 2000 was named by the PUBLIB as one of the top ten speakers in librarianship. An Air Force veteran (1983-1991), graduate of Barnard College, University of Illinois, and University of San Francisco Schneider is a technocrat who lives in Tallahassee, Florida.

Technology in Libraries: Essays in Honor of Anne Grodzins Lipow, ed. Roy Tennant. Lulu.com, 2008.

warded away the ocean chill with what appeared to be infinite combinations of jeans, turtlenecks, and clogs.

The Anne of my memory was a golden blur, a magnificent dress wafting around her like parachute silks as she floated full-tilt through the rosewood rooms of San Francisco's City Club, laughing as the music tinkled and the glitterati of librarianship drank wine and noshed and kibitzed and hundreds of faces turned her way, smiling at Anne ascendant. I can feel her warm arms clasping my shoulders and hear the breathy drama of her voice, which was given to italics and exclamation points—"But you two do *not* know one another? How could that *be*? Do you *like* the hor dieovers? But have you tasted *this* one? Isn't the music *amazing*?"—and again I am captivated, amazed as always not only by what she contributed to our profession, but by the sheer solar power of her presence, a woman so admired that her handwriting could be found on the whiteboards of the UC Berkeley Library a decade after her departure.

Dear Steve and Family,
I don't remember when I first met Anne, but I think it was on Telegraph Avenue where she was selling her design for a cookbook holder. ...

Posted by: Carol Starr | September 28, 2004 10:22 AM

In researching my friend and mentor, I briefly encountered an Anne I did not recognize, a woman of pleasant but otherwise unremarkable accomplishments and a forgettable lists of jobs. Anne arrived in Berkeley in 1957 with Art, her first husband, graduated from Berkeley's library school in 1961, and bore three children. Anne proceeded to spend her entire professional career in Berkeley, California, a duchy of limited growth (one of the few towns in the Bay Area to lose population in the last half-century) and famously liberal posturing. Anne kept her house on Oregon Street as a personal office and salon for receiving librarian visitors even after she had moved across the Bay to Belvedere and had largely retired from the publishing and consulting work that followed her retirement in 1992 after thirty years in the UC Berkeley library system, the only library she ever worked in. Even Anne's first decade at the library—as a bibliographer, then acquisitions librarian, and then cataloger—does not disturb the illusion of a demure woman carefully organizing the written word.

Appearances deceive; and everyone who knew Anne for more than a minute saw that Anne did not need to move somewhere else for "a change"; she simply changed where she was, over and over again.

> I can see Anne, leaning back in her chair, gazing out the windows of room 386 into the gray Berkeley morning sky toward Haviland Hall and the tall trees along the north edge of campus, wrapped up in thought and miles away from us all, as clearly as if it were yesterday. The dreamer and the immensely practical, both rolled up in Anne.
>
> Posted by: David Kessler at September 15, 2004 02:36 PM

From early in her career, Anne was an intellectual jackdaw. As she moved through UC Berkeley Library's departments for bibliography, acquisitions, cataloging, systems, and cooperative services, she gathered every bright gadget, idea, and person who came her way and used her booty to build nests great and small from which she hatched marvelous, sometimes insane, always inspired ideas. This was not limited to librarianship. In addition to everything else going on in her life—children, marriage (and divorce, and eventually remarriage), librarianship, labor organizing, free speech activism, feminism—Anne designed a redwood dreidel she crafted on Wednesday nights with her friends the Metzgers, and in the 1970s sold these dreidels on Shattuck Avenue so that Berkeley's good little liberal Jewish children would not have to spin a plastic top at Chanukah.

Anne was notorious for her serial crushes on small, "time-saving" household devices that she pushed on friends left and right. Anne, always prepared, carried two or three extra gadgets with her at all times, ranging from battery operated personal fans to apple peelers, mezzalunas, and hooks for eyeglasses. (One of her memorial services featured a table of her favorite gadgets, including several garlic presses, one of which her friends deemed actually useful.)

She wouldn't just sit quietly waiting for someone to approach her — no, she would proudly announce to every passerby "Look at how well it spins — here — try it." I remember once when some African American kids looked at her as somewhat crazy and responded "What's that? Why would anyone want it?" She immediately went into an enthusiastic pitch she thought they could relate to--it was a gambling device, and they could make a lot of money with it, and gave them its revolutionary history, and lo and behold she had another sale.

Posted by: Stephen Silberstein at September 16, 2004 12:23 PM

For all her love of gadgets and technology, Anne was not a girl geek or computer nerd. She had no interest in writing computer code, leaving that for Steve, the man who much later would become her second husband. (Steve worked with Anne in the Library Systems Office in the 1970s before departing to start the library software company, Innovative Interfaces.) Anne's less-technical perspective meant that she saw applications from the outside in, as gadgets that people used. Where programmers saw piles of machine code performing functions, she saw implications and outcomes.

One gadget was Anne understood early on was the software code written for the precursor to UC's Melvyl, one of the first online catalogs. Anne—always thinking about the user, always trying to connect the lumpish library to the people it served, always able to see the inventions inside the invention—quickly realized that the Ur-Melvyl system could take the data sent to it—the content of a typical catalog card—and process it in new and creative ways. Computers could be instructed to do the kind of searching—such as looking for words out of order, like "Jane Austen" instead of "Austen, Jane"—that was impossible in a card-based system.

Those scenes where Anne convinced programmers to exploit the flexibility of machine code are lost to time, but those of us who were around when Anne learned to cook, in the last ten years, can easily envision them.

Anne acquired her culinary skills the same way she accomplished everything else—by first declaring a state of emergency, and then wielding her formidable charm and powers of persuasion. "For most of her life she was enthusiastically proud that she didn't and indeed couldn't cook at all," said Steve. But in the late 1990s, Anne had an epiphany. Cooking—it's important! *Everyone* must to learn to cook! Especially Anne! Right *now*! Next came the seemingly unconquerable requirements: Anne would only learn recipes that could be prepared in ten minutes or less, even by a rank novice. Then Anne called in the experts, phoning everyone she knew with cooking skills and convincing them to give her cooking advice, recipes, and tips. Anne politely rejected advice that ran counter to her messianic vision, preferring to pull converts to her cause. In a city that bragged of "slow food," where every item on restaurant menus was qualified with heirloom-this and baby-that, Anne

---

Halibut Alaska (a favorite of Anne's)

4 pieces halibut steak, about 6 oz. each
1 C. dried bread crumbs
3/4 chopped onion
3/4 C. mayo
3/4 C. sour cream
Paprika

1. Preheat oven to 500 degrees.
2. Lightly grease a baking dish with butter.
3. Rinse the halibut in cold water and pat dry. Spread the bread crumbs on a paper towel. Dip both sides of the halibut in the bread crumbs and then place in the baking dish.
4. In a small bowl combine the onion, mayo, and sour cream. Spread over the halibut. Sprinkle with paprika.
5. Bake for 20 minutes.

Serves 4

Serve with roasted red potatoes and green beans.

From *On Your Own* by Alice Stern, Straight Arrow Press, 1996.

---

stoutly insisted that faster cooking was better. Then came the victory march as Anne, eyes gleaming with triumph, shamed her skeptics by conjuring up elegant ten-minute meals with the élan of a television cooking host. "You *see*? It only takes a *minute*! And only *six ingredients*!" And on her immaculately-set table she would slide four servings of the best cooking you had eaten in as long as you could remember.

From similar circumstances arose the Serials Keyword Index, developed in 1973 through code written by Walt Crawford, then working at UC Berkeley (he later moved on to the Research Libraries Group).

By current standards, the Serials Keyword Index was a quaint affair: a crude keyword catalog hoovered from the library's online serial holdings, comprised first of a massive printout on greenbar paper, and later of over 100 microfiche sorted neatly onto the yellow pasteboard wings of fiche readers available in the Library. (Through a later project of Anne's, more fiche readers would be spread throughout University departments.) But by the standards of information science in 1973, the Index was as important as if Anne had discovered fire (or learned to cook). Before the creation of the Index, if you wanted to find journals about education, you had to know that the *Los Angeles Business Educator* and *Studies in Education* existed; there was no other way to find them other than stumbling across their titles while searching print indexes to education literature, which were far from comprehensive. The Serials Keyword Index changed that: now a library user could use the term "Education" to find related journals—the librarian's equivalent of a ten-minute recipe.

Anne wanted it. Everyone needed it. Right *now*!

```
Sample listings for the keyword EDUCATION:

American Society for Engineering EDUCATION. Proceedings . . . . . . T61.S6   ENGI
(Business EDUCATION--California.) Los Angeles business educator . . F869.L8L849 BANC
Challenges in EDUCATION, Culture, and social welfare. Nuriel Hasan, Saiyid
(Studies in EDUCATION (new series) ; 1) Rosen Harold, ed. Language and   LC191.N85 MAIN
                                                          LB5.L56 ser.2 no.1  ED-P
```

Anne persuaded the systems department to generate the Index every two weeks, which with the glacially slow, primitive computers of that era was a major commitment of human and machine time. She then wrangled funding for the fiche production and related equipment required to display the fiche (I can see the meetings: Anne polite but passionate, librarians doubtful about the expense and staff time for something no one really *needed*), then convinced other librarians to use the Index and persuaded Richard Dougherty, the university librarian, to be its champion.

The path of librarianship is littered with the burned-out hulks of good ideas that lost airspeed and eventually crashed, but BAKER, a document delivery service that debuted in November, 1973, on the heels of the Serials Keyword Index, survives almost thirty years later not only essentially as Anne first designed it in 1973, but survives also, in a broader, more powerful sense, as a building block contributing to the growing profession-wide commitment to timely user service.

Anne had the unique quality of wearing several hats at the same time. She could walk into my office, as she did on numerous occasions, and give me hell about this or that, and then return a couple of hours later, in a completely different mindset, so that we could work together to develop an idea we were both interested in, like BAKER.

Posted by: Richard M. Dougherty | September 15, 2004 5:36 AM

Every large university now considers in-office document delivery to faculty a routine offering (usually now fee-based), but delivery and pickup of books and documents was almost unheard of in the 1970s, however obvious it seems in retrospect for a huge campus Balkanized into tiny feudal departments spread across dozens of woodsy, hilly acres—"an obstacle course," Anne called it—in an era when all knowledge was held captive in paper books and articles isolated in one physical facility. "Many people scoffed at the idea of such a thing," observed Howard Besser, then a library student working for Anne (and now a professor of information science). But Dougherty, a brisk university librarian with interesting ideas, was determined to see document delivery happen. "I had started a campus-wide delivery service while I was still at the University of Colorado in the late sixties. It was greatly appreciated by the faculty, but it was also controversial because a few faculty thought the money should be spent on books and journals, and not such a 'frivolous' service."

No doubt Anne's eyes lit up at the triple-threat challenge of something new, something controversial, and something that leveraged the automated services just emerging from the Systems Office. Berkeley faculty predicted failure and squawked at the cost—"Financially impossible," "Useless waste of resources," "Poor use of library funds" they grumped before BAKER rolled out—but Anne, at full tilt, smiled and kept going.

BAKER—named for the five-number extension that reached Anne and her team—was a Rube Goldberg device cobbled together from card catalogs, answering machines, hand-me-down library catalog microfiche from the Circulation department, and library vans in which her long-haired student assistants zoomed around Berkeley's tree-lined campus, plunking books and articles in faculty mailboxes. Despite its stone-soup beginnings, BAKER was soon an enormously popular service that helped rejuvenate the library's presence on campus, much as coffee bars and free wifi have helped pick up the image of this decade's libraries. Soon faculty members could not remember that they had not wanted document delivery, and by 1975 they were willing to pay for it out of their departmental funds.

"For the first time in four and a half years I've been at Berkeley, I now feel that the Main Library is a usable research resource rather than the hindrance it has so frequently seemed to be," admitted one academic to Anne. Other faculty members, enamored of door-to-door delivery, suddenly discovered the value of BAKER, arguing that in "sheer economic terms" due to time saved on trips to the library, it was an invaluable, indispensable service. BAKER was a hit with the Library staff, who soon realized that BAKER ramped up their status among the faculty, who as Anne later wryly noted were "amazed at the library's ability to locate materials they themselves had been unable to find after long searches."

Early 1981 was not a lighthearted time for librarians at UC Berkeley. Library staff were fractious and anxious; change was afoot, and many did not like it. For years the library administration—held under sway by a "vocal section of the staff,"[1] as Anne later baldly stated in an article in *Library Journal* — had shied away from closing the card catalog and moving to an online catalog. But the cost of filing card catalogs had risen to $100,000 in 1980 — big dollars in those days — and UC Berkeley had a backlog of 125,000 unfiled catalog cards. The final blow came from the rules changes in AACR2, published in 1978, that could not reasonably be implemented in a library the size of UC Berkeley without turning to automation.

In the fall of 1980, the Library administration had decreed the closure of the card catalog; then, under pressure from resistant staff, the administration reversed its decision; then finally accepted the inevitable and pushed the library on an irrevocable course towards change.

```
QUESTION:          What's wrong with cards?
WRONG ANSWER 1:    We're trying to conserve paper.
WRONG ANSWER 2:    Do you have any idea how hard
                   it is to get someone to punch
                   holes in 3x5 cards?
WRONG ANSWER 3:    They're terrible! They
                   multiply in the night and
                   cause all our filing errors.
RIGHT ANSWER:
     Cards work well for small and medium-
sized libraries but when you are dealing
with the cards for over 5 million books,
things get a lot stickier.  Berkeley spends
almost $150,000 a year just to file cards
in its many catalogs and making corrections
to the card catalog is an almost insurmountable
and never-ending task.  This along with the
changes in cataloging rules that will start
in January 1981 caused the library to
consider a more efficient method of producing
and changing catalog records.  A computerized
catalog was the obvious answer since it
allows for relatively easy corrections and
maintenance and there is no card filing
involved.

     #########################
To fiche or not to fiche - that is no
     longer the question.
     #########################
                8
```

Anne brought her light touch to the tense atmosphere. "Change prepares the ground for revolution," she wrote with tongue firmly in cheek in *Quotations from Chairman Joe*. This small, pocket-sized book—another Anne Gadget—became the doxology for the Catalog Instruction Group, 28 librarians known with poetic license as the "Gang of 24."

Quotations—perhaps the first-ever handbook for using an online catalog--is a wee red pamphlet perfect for tucking in a skirt pocket-- yet another example of Anne's handy gadgets. *Quotations* is so well-known in the Berkeley crowd that a generation of librarians can cite examples of the "wrong answers" librarians were advised not to provide patrons: "If we didn't make it hard for you, we'd be out of a job"; "That's for me to know and you to

---

[1] Fortunately, this never happens any more.

find out"; and "Don't pay any attention—nothing's changed." It was a tough time, but a small red book helped.

Anne's experiences with BAKER and the Serials Keyword Index lead Anne to a natural conclusion: Berkeley's faculty did not know how to use the Library. So in the 1980s Anne designed training classes tailored to faculty needs, and called these classes Faculty Seminars "so that faculty wouldn't be turned off," remembered Dougherty, who added, "There used to be a common expression: 'What can you tell a Berkeley faculty member? Answer: Very little.' Anne wanted to avoid the appearance of talking down to the faculty. I think she was successful."

Anne's appointment as Education Officer in 1982—yet another new position created based on her groundwork in the area of staff and user education—only accelerated the Library's automation process.

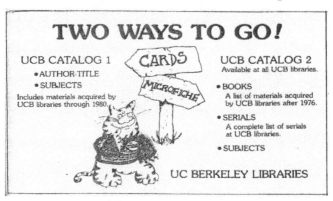

I first met Anne when she came to help us while I was running the Apple Library. We wanted to create a series of workshops in the early 90's on using the Internet. We proudly showed her our course outlines and marketing materials, and in her wonderful, kind way she told us to toss away what we'd done and start over. And of course, she was absolutely right! ... We are all incredibly lucky to have had her in our lives.

Posted by: Monica Ertel at September 12, 2004 02:24 PM

She not only taught library staff how to use automated systems, she proselytized freely about why, and with typical good humor and creativity, conditioned Library staff to be automation-friendly and to be apostles of access for their users. Humorous, proto-Garfieldian characters such as CatFiche graced educational posters Anne produced, illustrated by UC librarian and artist Gary Handman; "advice columns" providing comfort to librarians who missed the card catalog appeared in the *CU News*; and peppy, funny posters—in an academic library, no less—helped librarians and patrons alike navigate the complex new waters of library automation.

The 1980s were when Anne developed her workshop, "Public Service under Pressure," designed to help librarians handle "common pressure situations" faced on public service desks, such as angry patrons or long lines during busy hours. Once again, a message that might have stuck in some craws went down easily once Anne spun it with her typical humor and enthusiasm. Anne at first held these classes on her personal time for a local public library system, which suggests she may have had to prove the value of these classes before the library agreed to include them in the curriculum; but once word-of-mouth began about these classes, UC Berkeley not only held these courses regularly until Anne retired but sent Anne and her good friend and colleague Sue Calpestri on road trips around the country to share UC's skills with other libraries—the "circuit preacher" speaking/consulting route that some librarians have turned into 21st-century careers.

> Ann flew through life.
>
> Posted by: Suzanne Riess | September 15, 2004 6:22 PM

I met Anne in her "retirement," when she was the publisher of Library Solutions Press. In a column for *American Libraries* I wrote that "everything Library Solutions Press publishes is stupendously useful," and Anne used that heartfelt blurb throughout the life of her publishing house. (When I first met Anne, in fact, I thought she was just a nice librarian with a vanity press.)

Anne, as a publisher, was much like Anne the librarian. She had started her publishing business in 1993 for a typical Anne reason: traditional publishers were far too damn slow to meet the swelling demand for her Internet handbooks. Beginning with *Crossing the Internet Threshold*—one of the first clear, librarian-oriented guides to using the 'net—Library Solutions Press proceeded to be the premier publishing house for library-oriented Internet training manuals, filling a crucial publishing gap during the 1990s.

Anne was not just any publisher. She used union labor, paid her authors monthly, and bought back unsold books; not only that, but her books were handsome, well-edited, and copyedited to a fare-thee-well. A couple of years before she died, Anne decided to get out of the publishing business, and my favorite Post-It of all time is Anne's uncharacteristically caustic note to me fuming that she would never write for that publisher again. Sadly, she was correct.

Throughout her last years, at her swank parties at San Francisco's City Club or her New Year's receptions at her home in Tiburon, Anne was a hostess who "had the fantastic grace to treat each guest as if you were the only guest," as her friend Maryll Telegdy remembered at one of Anne's memorial services. No doubt Anne's graciousness helped the forces for automation prevail in the 1970s and 1980s; by all accounts, she paid close attention to every person involved in the change process, explaining herself exhaustively. As Calpestri recalls, if someone didn't agree with Anne, Anne reacted as if it was because she had explained the situation incorrectly. "She'd be trying to make a point and the person wouldn't get it. Anne would say, 'Give me another chance.' She would just keep trying; she never had emotional vocabulary to be impatient with others."

####

Seeing her name in the *Chronicle* yesterday, I learned that somewhere inside me there had always been the secret hope and expectation that Anne would live to be at least ninety-five and that the world would be better off because she was somewhere among us, serving the greater public good. Now that burden shifts to those of us still walking the planet.

Posted by: John Truxaw | September 13, 2004 11:31 AM

I repeatedly tried to end this farewell to Anne on that note, but I was distracted by the ghostly image of her handwriting on the whiteboard at the Teaching Library. In researching the history of Anne Lipow, I knew ahead of time that with Anne's death we had lost an important primary source for understanding her life—Anne herself. But in my librarian hubris I was confident that research could fill in any blanks that human subjects could not. My confidence began dwindling when I dug through databases, hunting for accounts of BAKER and Melvyl and early automation, only to discover that the online indexes for the scientific literature of our profession stop in the mid-1970s at best, and that is assuming we can be satisfied with citation indexes; full-text articles do not go back farther than the 1980s in most cases. I was able to turn to the print indexes, but I had to drive forty miles to do so, as Stanford, the university closest to me at the time, no longer carries the print indices for *Library Literature* (and because Stanford is a private school, its Library would not give me access to their physical holdings without an "institutional" pass, which I had no means to procure).

Deep in the quiet and orderly bowels of Doe Library, I felt consternation and dismay at the tenuous quality of nearly fifty years' worth of *CU Library News*, a weekly newsletter of the UC Berkeley library system (published electronically since 1994). I had spent many hours reading several decades' worth of the *CU News* to garner facts and confirm dates—a strategy I did not choose, but which was forced upon me because the only index to the print version of this newsletter, a card index, no longer exists. Based on my research, *CU News* is the most significant historical record of this period of librarianship (and of its leaders, such as Anne), but it is a record that will soon be as lost as the libraries of Alexandria if we do not take heed. Though I gingerly tiptoed through the fading buckram volumes, I felt history slipping through my hands. Yellowing pages slid out (of course I put them back!); old bindings creaked; and I saw ink fading and paper crumbling, as if Anne's years

13

in the Library were a dream about to slip from my mind upon awakening. For some documents, such as *Quotations*, I used my personal "grey literature" sources—begging copies from Anne's friends and family—rather than interlibrary loan because I hesitated to send the lone circulating copy of an item into the wilds of the U.S. postal service.

Every time Anne trained, she published materials, as well, from tiny red books to large, handsome training guides on the Internet. In all this writing and publishing, in all of her guidebooks and printing and colorful signs and clever pocket-sized guides, it is as if Anne was sending us a message, moving through a room in a swift golden blur, reminding us of our legacy.

Anne's work was too important, there is far too much yet to understand, to let it crumble away in the slow forgotten fires that consume the paper record. This must change: we must digitize and make globally available everything related to that era—*UC Library News, Quotations from Chairman Joe*, and every bit of grey literature we can scrabble from the echoing halls of the past. We need to be able to carry Anne with us in our pocket, to be able to continue to see the ghost of her writing on the walls of our profession. She has been patiently, enthusiastically, and with great humor telling us how to do this for over forty years; it would honor her memory if we showed her we were listening.

##

Thanks to University of San Francisco librarians Debbie Malone, Penny Scott, and Sherise Kimura, and the nameless gentleman at the Periodicals Desk who jimmied open the stuck microfiche drawer, for their above-and-beyond research assistance with this portrait.

I often think of her when I need to be bold.

Posted by: John Ober | September 13, 2004 4:57 PM

Partnering For The Future
Helen Hayes

Anne Lipow's approach to life was always positive. While others might be marshalling arguments for "why not", she would be encouraging "how to" approaches to meeting organizational challenges. One of the first times I met Anne she was wearing a T-shirt with "I Crossed the Internet Threshold" emblazoned across the front. At the time this was a serious challenge to the group that she was about to enthuse into doing just that. It seems therefore appropriate that this paper should raise some challenging issues for libraries that Anne would have considered to be exciting opportunities and how libraries can address these complexities in our institutions.

All higher education institutions are undergoing significant adaptations to the increasingly global, knowledge-based economies in which they operate. Competition to attract the best students and staff on an international scale is growing, and league tables have become increasingly important for gaining and maintaining competitive edge. Vice Chancellors with business experience are entering University leadership where once only senior academics would be found. Funding over and above that provided through funded student places is increasingly important and income generated through fees, research grants and other business initiatives help to make up an ever-larger proportion of total funds, to support innovation and meet recurrent costs.

Helen Hayes recently returned to Australia having served as Vice Principal for Knowledge Management and Librarian to the University at the University of Edinburgh. Ms. Hayes held a number of key executive positions in Australia including president of the Council of Australian University Librarians from 1998 to 2002, and prior to this she was President of the Australian Council of Libraries and Information Services. Ms. Hayes is currently a member of the Stanford University Library and Information Resources Advisory Council. In recognition of her work on behalf of libraries in Australia, Ms Hayes was awarded a fellowship of the Australia Information and Library Association and received national recognition by being named Australian Business Woman of the Year in the Corporate and Government sector in 1999.

Technology in Libraries: Essays in Honor of Anne Grodzins Lipow, ed. Roy Tennant. Lulu.com, 2008.

This places increasing pressure on all support group services to justify the resources they use, and this is nowhere more pressing than for library and information services.

In addition, technological advances and ICT has put the 'e' into everything. Thirty years ago the online industry was in the hands of six companies and a few government agencies, whereas technology today is in the hands of virtually everyone who wants it. Libraries have been able to move with, and even keep ahead of, this tidal wave, but it is becoming harder to maintain the pace of change while at the same time driving down overall costs. Keeping momentum for existing services and being innovative for introducing new services is a real challenge in a resource-constrained environment. At the same time library users have become increasingly proficient consumers of information and are more demanding of the services that libraries provide. Internet time has created demand for 24x7x365 and information that is "a zero click away". Students attitudes are being influenced by changing patterns of work, as many must help to meet the costs of their own education by working part-time, and this creates an even greater demand for easy, flexible, anytime delivery. Not only are we being challenged by our funders, and by our users, but there are additional trends that are significantly changing the fabric of our business, causing libraries to re-think and re-align their business focus. Some of these trends are:

- The emergence of Google and Google Scholar late in 2004 which is now tapping literature that was less easy to access in the past and is proving to be a great benefit to researchers. It has replaced the library as the first port of call for enquiry.
- Mass digitization by Google of some 10 million items from the libraries of Stanford, Oxford, Harvard, Michigan and the New York Public Library is bringing enormous quantities of high quality information online. Projects led by Amazon, Yahoo and Microsoft are beginning to create the global virtual library.
- Social software such as blogs and wikis are making available huge quantities of free information in areas of interest to many library users. Communities of practice are forming without reference to

traditional boundaries around common themes and issues in an economy of "give and take".

- Disintermediation as a business strategy being pursued by commercial information suppliers to reduce costs and achieve speedier delivery to end users.
- 'Pay per view' and 'on-demand' publishing is increasingly breaking information down into chunks available anywhere, anytime at an affordable price.
- The falling cost of computing, and the pervasive nature of the digital environment are now the norm for the developed world and 'e' will soon disappear as a prefix from our language.

In this context, the question arises as to the value libraries will be adding for their stakeholders in five or ten years time, when these trends alongside providers that have deeper pockets, greater access to expertise and more ability to innovate, take over a greater part of the cyberspace in which libraries have been the primary players. Anne Lipow would have clearly seen this as an opportunity to improve our business in new and exciting ways.

Setting aside for the moment the positive arguments that relate to our great traditions embodied in our special and rare collections and traditional user services, libraries have a further major advantage over external suppliers of information. Libraries are in the unique position of being close to, and able to best understand, the businesses of their academy, and a library's competitive advantage is to demonstrate to users and institutional leaders that all of the services they provide clearly enhance the business of the academic enterprise. To achieve this advantage, alignment of all library services to academic strategy must be demonstrated whether re-shelving books or undertaking a complex search, and library staff need to be made aware of the contribution that their work makes to the overall academic mission of the institution. To understand academic needs, both strategically and operationally, libraries must work at several levels. Operationally, this will be closely with user groups at the coal face conducting research into user needs, guiding users to information resources, customizing resources to their teaching and research needs and helping members of the University to be more effective and more innovative in their work. Strategically, they must understand the future directions, research priorities and areas of development that will be important to support building greater capability by aligning resources and services to high-level priorities. Libraries need to engage with the leadership thinking in academic departments, Schools and Colleges and other support groups so that choices can be made that relate clearly to key areas of planning and development. This requires not only engagement by subject specialists and systems staff, but also by trusted library leaders who are able to discuss issues around academic mission, goals, and priorities and to clearly articulate this context and how it influences library resource allocation. All too often engagement with academics has been around fair distribution of resources allocated in a collegial way that may appease many but not be supporting key institutional goals and targets.

The current model of academic engagement relies heavily on the excellent work of subject librarians and the available time of the senior managers, but given the strategic importance of building partnership with academic and student groups there is immense value to be gained by appointing senior staff who are primarily responsible for customer relationships in order to develop these relationships further. These staff would be expected to combine the skills of marketing, business analysis and service delivery, and possess outstanding personal attributes that would include for being innovative, outwardly-facing, team players with broad knowledge and the ability to influence and effect change. Senior customer relationship managers would engage with academics in planning and decision-making, while also being a key part of library planning and resource allocation, acting as the primary interface between academic leadership in colleges, and library leadership. Such individuals may be appointed from an academic area or from the library itself, recognizing that each would bring different strengths to this post. It is the ability to understand academic needs and align library services to these as they develop that is important. Nevertheless if a customer relationship manager is drawn from an academic environment, excellent induction into the full range of library services will be required.

In an increasingly digital world, human interactions are themselves increasingly important for achieving a common understanding for all involved concerning the range and depth of services that libraries provide, and for showing how these services support and enhance the work of the institution in teaching, learning, research and knowledge transfer. Personal interactions enhance the prospect of engagement and creating greater mutual understanding, which enables librarians to work in partnership with students and staff to discover new and better avenues for enhancing their work, through the resources and services the library provides. By creating regular dialogue with academic colleagues at both the strategic and operational levels that informs library and information support, librarians are more likely to be viewed as valued peers, and as such to discover new ways of operating that are more satisfying and challenging than previously. That is, libraries are, or need to be, in "mission shift" from being providers and supporters to partners and colleagues in the academic enterprise.

By being closely integrated with the academic enterprise and by contributing clearly to the core mission and objectives of the institution, libraries are likely to receive more sympathetic consideration during institutional budget reviews. For example, a collaboration between the student body and the library at the University of Edinburgh in 2004 led to a number of library initiatives being accelerated through the university's planning and budgeting processes. This followed a joint study involving students, academic and library staff to consider student needs over a 5 year period and the recommendations received support from academic and support groups based on the highly collaborative approach which aims to improve the student experience in a range of ways. As a result hours of service were increased, new electronic resources were considerably enhanced and there is a major project to redevelop the Main Library by redesigning learning spaces for interactive and group learning, and for quiet study, with a new café where reading, texting and coffee go together.

An extract from this 2004 report provides a flavor of how students viewed the way library services should be developed.

"Students' work patterns are changing. At the same time as having an instant message conversation you could be searching online, reading an e-journal, checking your email and writing your essay! Understanding the way students want to work, and providing them with the ability to work the way they want is synonymous with ensuring that students are efficient and effective learners who are able to manage knowledge when and how they want it. Different types of students require different methods to learn, support needs to be based on the principle of 'plug and play'[1].

The ability to understand the particular needs of customer groups and to engage with users of all kinds moves libraries from being provider-centric to user-centric; delivering services from the perspective of researcher, teacher and learner, while recognizing that within these groups there is limited homogeneity. In a user-centric model we provide services to support the function that is being performed and not by creating services around existing library work group structures. The model therefore works best where collaboration and shared working is part of the library and information culture and where communication is well developed across internal and external work boundaries.

In practice the user-centric service model when applied to particular library programs, is closely aligned to the mission and objectives of the institution and reflects the needs and aspirations of key user communities. For example, when applied to a collection strategy it will reflect the primary mission whether the focus of the institution is primarily on research, teaching or both, and how these should be addressed reflecting in the objectives a clear understanding of those areas of teaching or research that are high impact and high priority including those areas that provide competitive advantage. For a research-intensive university, high priority areas are more likely to need deep and rich collections complemented by esoteric resources, primary sources, special collections and well developed complementary services, such as subject portals and repositories, to provide particular advantage to researchers. In the mission-driven model no collection should be acquired or exploited in isolation from the value it provides to research or teaching, and every

---

[1] Sarah Nicholson, Vice President Research, Edinburgh University Students Association

opportunity should be taken to obtain best value from that resource. For example, an international team of experts led by the University of Edinburgh has produced numerous research papers as a result of the high resolution digitization of the most important of Christine de Pizan's surviving presentation manuscripts, the British Library's Harley MSS 4431 (c.1413), exposing the lavishly illuminated manuscript to greater interpretation and analysis.

The information seeking habits of researchers vary greatly and where science, technology and medicine (STM) relies almost entirely on electronic information, in the Humanities and Social Sciences (HSS) a hybrid environment is still common. Not only will researchers in STM require digital print material, but also data which are important for areas such as informatics, astronomy, biology, crystallography and others. If libraries wish to become strategic partners with academics in STM they must engage in e-science, data storage and preservation as part of the services they provide. There are many sources of information beyond more generally acknowledged library resources sometimes held in departmental files or laboratories or possibly held elsewhere but may only be known to a few enthusiastic researchers. Many of these resources require better management whether they form part of the library's collections or not. Professional judgment is needed to guide appropriate identification, acquisition, management and retention of the range of information resources an institution creates as part of its normal business.

Subject and format repositories add value to collections by offering access to a wider and deeper range of materials for teaching and for research. For example, researchers and teachers alike at the University of Edinburgh have access to repositories produced by the library on the basis of its own collections which can be complemented by digitized treasures held in other collections in order to compose important virtual collections. Edinburgh currently offers the Walter Scott Digital Archive, for example, which is based on the extensive Corson Collection of Walter Scott material held in Special Collections. Other examples include the Baillie Papers, digitized from the collection of John Baillie, an early 20th century Free Church minister and leading theologian, which are an important resource for researchers in church history.   The Charting the Nation image collection of over 3,500 high-resolution images includes a wide variety of maps, atlases and other bound books, together with important manuscript and printed texts relating to the geography and mapping of Scotland from 1550 to 1740 and beyond.

These repositories of digital material represent curated collections of value to the University community but also to scholarship more generally.

The library is also working through a program of digitization of discrete items, from its own collections, from those of the Museums and Galleries of the University, and from academic Schools, in order to provide general-purpose repositories.   The most prominent of these is our repository of images, which is currently used in the teaching of fine art, art history and architecture, but in time as the repository grows it will also support teaching in medicine and across the range of science and engineering subjects.   Its images are restricted for use within the University, and they can be exported for use by individual academics in creating their own customized collections to support courses, with image management and presentation software also provided by the library.   In the same way, 'born digital' material can also be stored in repositories now provided by the library.   Teachers can draw on re-usable digital learning objects via the LORE (Learning Objects Repository for Edinburgh University).

In addition researchers can access the public outputs of the whole University academic community, as well as deposit and retrieve their own research outputs, having confidence that these will be preserved for the longer term.   To this end, many libraries are now developing Open Access Archives. This exposes material that may not be placed in a refereed journal and also helps to mitigate the high prices demanded of libraries by some publishers for the material that their own researchers produce.   In many cases open access publication in local repositories satisfies research funding bodies who require that publicly funded research is made more widely available.   The Edinburgh Research Archive fulfills a strategic need for the University as a digital repository containing the outputs of the University of Edinburgh.   It contains full text theses and dissertations, book chapters, journal pre-prints and peer reviewed pre-prints, and has value as a record of the University's intellectual outputs as well as being useful for reporting and review.

As mentioned previously library strategy needs to address the broader university information environment and include collections that are neither acquired nor held in the library, such as the extensive local cultural assets held in galleries and museums, or even in the office spaces of staff members. Librarians need to partner with archives and records staff to ensure that coordination over the range of information assets is achieved.

The greatest value from all information investments can only be achieved when relevant information that is held locally or elsewhere is exposed to the right person in the right context. Understanding the needs of each discipline and balancing collections development against institutional priorities, building areas of academic excellence while acknowledging historical strengths does not necessarily mean that a collections or services budget should be evenly spread across subject areas without differentiating and rebalancing as appropriate against institutional priorities. In addition, the most effective collection strategy does not necessarily rely on building the largest collection but recognizes that relevance and differentiation are essential for supporting institutional goals and objectives. No single library can purchase everything it wants or house everything it requires in perpetuity so collaborations that achieve broader access, more efficient resource use and better service delivery need to be explored and developed with other information providers. As researchers are expected to assume ever more administrative tasks, services such as customized alerts to newly discovered material, federated searching across multiple and appropriate datasets, being able to track and trail as needs dictate are services that can provide highly sophisticated information delivery to teachers and researchers, enabling them to be more effective in their work. Libraries are increasingly adding value not just by collecting and acquiring knowledge, but by contextualizing it thereby increasing opportunities for researchers to develop new knowledge. Understanding the needs of academics, and providing better ways of supporting their educational aims, gives strategic advantage to the university and recognition to libraries for understanding these priorities.

By moving from provider-centric to user-centric services, there are opportunities to enhance the business of the University that requires coordination and support across different service groups while working in partnership with academic colleagues. For example, distance-learning provision requires support from IT, e-learning, library and student services staff. IPR advice is required in a range of areas including repositories, e-learning, and knowledge transfer; information skills development requires collaboration across libraries, IT, e-learning and academic groups. Research requires support from libraries working with IT colleagues, and so on. Knowledge management is a shared environment and working in this environment involves working collaboratively to achieve user requirements based on strategic institutional needs above local agendas but where many opportunities exist for the library to take a lead coordinating role. Partnerships and collaboration that embed library services into the very fabric of the institutional mission is essential for achieving successful outcomes and recognition from academics and university administrators.

Traditional university structures are breaking down and lines of command are blurring. Librarians will be greatly valued for their ability to partner and knowing when to allow others to lead recognizing when well managed "followership" is appropriate. Users used to a virtual world expect services where support groups join to provide seamless service interactions without barriers created by structures. Any failure to recognize new roles could result in marginalization or disintermediation as our users seek more effective and flexible solutions to their information needs. The challenge of being able to respond to the demands of business priorities is to become more nimble and effective in moving resources to achieve greater alignment to institutional priorities, breaking down established silos, and viewing our work from the perspective of what value we are able to add to the work of our users rather than what we do. By taking the user-centric, more strategic approach to our work across library and organizational boundaries it becomes clear where changes are needed and where re-purposing is appropriate. This approach requires that serious attention is paid to efficiency gains, including outsourcing and self help services, so that resources can be more effectively applied to high value, high profile user services that are well regarded. Understanding client needs requires excellent liaison at both the strategic leadership level and at the coalface, combined with market influence. Recognizing that library users have different requirements based on research or teaching orientation, discipline, background or previous experience;

market research is needed to ensure that services are assigned to user requirements within the broader context of departmental and institutional priorities.

Libraries are facing many challenges in an environment that is critically aware of business needs and how well they can meet and exceed expectations will depend on how effectively contribution to business success can be demonstrated.

Background Reading

Mass Digitization: Implications for Information Policy Report from "Scholarship and Libraries in transition": a Dialogue about impacts of Mass Digitization Projects Symposium held in March 10-11, 2006. Ann Arbor MI: University of Michigan.

US National Commission on Libraries and Information Science (NCLIS) May 9, 2006.

Campbell, Jerry D. "Changing a Cultural Icon: The Academic Library as Virtual Destination," *Educause Review*, January/February 2006, p.16-30.

Chester, Timothy M., "A Roadmap For IT Leadership and the Next Ten Years," *Educause Quarterly*, Number 2, 2006, p.56-60.

Keller, Michael A., "Whether academic Information Services in the Perfect Storm of the Early 21st Century?" Presentation delivered at 8th International Bielefeld Conference, Bielefeld (Germany).

University of Edinburgh Knowledge Management Strategic Plan, 2005-2008 http://www.kmstrategy.ed.ac.uk/ .

Nicholson, Sarah, http://www.kmstrategy.ed.ac.uk/EUSA_Paper1.pdf .

The Teaching Library: Rethinking Library Services
Ellen Meltzer

From Undergraduate Library to Teaching Library

The James K. Moffitt Undergraduate Library, opened in the fall of 1970 on the University of California, Berkeley campus, was conceived and completed during a period of escalating democracy on college campuses with undergraduate libraries as one example. Prior to this period of student activism, undergraduates at large universities were traditionally denied access to the stacks of the research collections. To get their hands on books, they had to fill out a slip and request that the books or bound journals they wanted to read be paged from the stacks. Students could go through a lengthy process of identifying items from the enormous card catalog (taking up two massive rooms), filling out forms for each desired title, standing in a long line, and waiting, only to discover that what they had paged was not what they really needed.

In a growth economy, emerging spirit of openness and free speech, several large university campuses built new undergraduate libraries.[2] Between 1960-1970, the Universities of British Columbia, Missouri, Wisconsin, Indiana, Miami, Pennsylvania, Cornell, Southern California, Notre Dame, Pennsylvania State, Alberta, Texas, Washington, Johns Hopkins, Boston, Florida, SUNY-Albany, Stanford, Ohio State, Bowling Green, Cleveland State, Miami University, UC San Diego, Michigan State, Pittsburgh, Texas A&M, Hawaii, North Carolina, Duke, Iowa State, Nebraska, UC Berkeley,

Ellen Meltzer is Information Services Manager at the California Digital Library (CDL). She is responsible for overseeing user services for resources and services managed by the CDL. Prior to this position, she served as Senior Associate for Education, Usability and Outreach at the CDL. She came to the CDL from the UC Berkeley Library in 2001, where she served in a variety of positions, most recently as Head of the Teaching Library.

Technology in Libraries: Essays in Honor of Anne Grodzins Lipow, ed. Roy Tennant. Lulu.com, 2008.

---

[2] Person, Roland Conrad. *A New Path: Undergraduate Libraries at United States and Canadian Universities, 1949-1987.* New York, Greenwood Press: 1988.

and Chicago founded undergrad libraries. (And Pennsylvania and SUNY-Albany closed them in the same period.) (Harvard, Illinois, UCLA, Michigan and others had established undergraduate libraries as far back as 1949.[3]) Yet more undergraduate libraries continued to be built.

Undergraduates were perceived to have special requirements. In the Main Stack of the Research Library, books and journals were interfiled; English and languages other than English — over 60% of Cal's collections — were all found next to each other on the shelves. It could be difficult, for example, to find a simple English language version of *The Doll's House*. The original Doe stacks were crammed, dark, dusty and even frightening; an earthquake disaster site if there ever was one. These conditions and the feeling among some faculty that undergrads were a mass of the "great unwashed" played a part in moving them away from the true research collections to the undergrad library.

The new undergraduate libraries would serve the needs of this group of activist students with open stacks, collections of the "best books" selected for them by librarians focusing on undergraduates; separate reserve collections; and specialized reference and instruction services. Undergraduate libraries were often served by their own separate technical service operations.

In addition to doing reference and collection management, librarians from Moffitt Undergraduate Library at UC Berkeley taught an undergraduate research methodologies class, Bibliography 1, each quarter through UC Berkeley's Library School. Up to twenty-five sessions of the class were taught each quarter until 1985. In addition to a reference desk staffed for many years from 8:00 am to 10:00 pm most days, this was the primary method Moffitt Librarians reached Cal's undergraduates with bibliographic instruction, as it was referred to at the time.[4]

---

[3] Ibid, p.49.

[4] For more information about Bibliography 1, see Wheeler, Helen Rippier. *For-Credit, Undergraduate, Bibliographic Instruction Courses in the University of California System With Consideration of the Berkeley Campus' Bibliography 1 Course-Program's History As a Model.* [Alexandria, Va.?]: ERIC Document Reproduction Service, 1986.

Forming the Teaching Library

Fast forward to 1992. The Library had a new University Librarian[5], a new vision, and transformative technologies to understand and integrate into student learning. It was the year before Anne Lipow published *Rethinking Reference In Academic Libraries*. And rethink we did. Increasingly, students were conducting research from the comfort of their residence halls and apartments, as online resources burgeoned in the digital library space.

At the University of California system, the Division of Library Automation (DLA) was making impressive progress in library automation and access to an array of online information resources. Over the period of a few years, databases came on line with citations or full text via the Melvyl Catalog system: Magazine Index, National Newspaper Index, Computer Database, MEDLINE, INSPEC, ABI/Inform, ERIC, GeoRef, Hispanic American Periodicals Index (HAPI), Legi-Slate, PsycINFO and more.

It became possible to download citations from Melvyl into personal citation management software (e.g., EndNote, ProCite). An impressive and seamless online interlibrary loan service dubbed Request was launched in 1993. Library users were greeting these new online databases and services with amazement and enthusiasm. Less and less (and now, even less and less!), did students have to come into the physical space of the library to conduct their research. "During her keynote address at the *Ninth Australasian Information Online and On Disc Conference* in 1999, Ann [sic] Grodzins Lipow made the now oft quoted observation, 'Rather than thinking of our users as remote, we should instead recognize that it is we who are remote from our users.'"[6] The die of the virtual library was cast.

Librarians and library staff were no longer envisioned to be passive recipients of students approaching the reference desk, but as teachers who sought out students in the classroom. UC Berkeley's Teaching Library (TLIB) was born. Part of the reframing of the library was to liberate library

---

[5] Actually, there were two new University Librarians in a short period of time who supported the Teaching Library concept: Dorothy Gregor, from 1992-1994 and Peter Lyman, 1994-1998.

[5] Mizzy, Danianne. 2004. The Virtual Reference Librarian's Handbook (review). *Portal: Libraries and the Academy*. 4, no.1, p. 157-158.

[6] Taken from initial Program Coordinator job descriptions.

staff from the tasks of operation managers, spending the bulk of their energies on facilities problems, for example, and instead to refocus their intellectual energies on teaching and imagining how students could integrate research skills smoothly into their academic lives. In large part, TLIB was an extension of Moffitt Undergraduate Library, but envisioned in a new way. By giving this service a new name and identity, attention was drawn to the Teaching Library both on campus and beyond. TLIB had a new logo, a black and white book atop a computer, and lapel (or backpack) buttons were made to celebrate its birth. The creation of this new unit resulted in a spirited, cohesive group of enthusiastic library professionals, from the administrative assistant to the head.

There were several bold moves in imagining the Teaching Library. One was its organizational structure. TLIB was comprised of a group of program coordinators who were both professional librarians and high level library assistants. Those in the library assistant series were teamed with a librarian. While all the positions were filled internally to the library, staff had to apply for the positions, identifying themselves as being passionate about teaching. As a result, TLIB staff clearly relished developing curriculum, working in tandem with faculty, undergraduate and graduate students, and campus student services staff.

Requiring interested staff library-wide to apply for TLIB positions (including those already working in Moffitt Library) resulted in a new and surprising mix of staff coming from unexpected corners of the Library, such as Interlibrary Loan and the Biosciences Library Circulation department. This trend continued in later years, when TLIB attracted and nurtured staff from the Acquisitions Department and Library Conservation. Our ads (if we had had them) would have read: "One qualification needed: love of teaching. Will train."

Program Coordinators were hired, librarians and library assistants. They were responsible for "providing leadership in developing, implementing and evaluating course-integrated, stand alone and adjunct information literacy programs aimed at students and faculty."[7] They coordinated various aspects of teaching and learning, such as setting up instructional sessions for large

---

[7] Taken from initial Program Coordinator job descriptions.

undergraduate research courses; coordinating tours; doing outreach to non-library campus units responsible for undergraduate services (e.g., Student Learning Center, Reentry Student Program); Web and Web-based instruction; faculty seminars. As first head of the Teaching Library, I tried to instill a can-do attitude within the staff; an atmosphere where the first answer would always be "yes." (A very Anne Lipow-esque trait, I might add.) As a result, "interesting" projects came our way:

- Developing and teaching gopher and the first campus World Wide Web classes.
- Constructing a cross-discipline database of students' dissertation topics in the social sciences and humanities so that campus graduate students could be aware of others researching similar topics in fields other than their own (e.g., across history, sociology, and political science), and share ideas.
- Creating the overall site design of a project using DynaText as an interface for transliterating scanned images of Catalan Medieval manuscripts for a UC Berkeley – UC Irvine distance learning course.
- Setting up a server and training for graduate students for the UC Berkeley Technology and Humanities Project.
- Creating a pilot program using California Heritage materials from the UC Berkeley Bancroft Library to work with local area K-12 teachers and students through UC Berkeley's Interactive University project.

User research from the beginning

In addition to Program Coordinators, a half-time User Research coordinator position was created. The User Research Coordinator, the original posting stated, "will play an important role in defining and classifying users into logical segments, defining and tracking their evolving needs, aiding in suggesting and testing service concepts, and bringing new information products and services to the Library in a timely fashion."[8] This position would be responsible for conducting user studies, such as surveys, focus groups, one-on-one interviews, and usability studies with UC Berkeley students and faculty.[9] The goal of creating such a position in the Library was to ensure that users drove the direction of library services. [10] Creating this position was prescient, in many ways. It pre-dated the creation of many such positions in academic libraries, and has proven to be a rich information resource for the campus and to the library profession. [11]

Other services as part of TLIB

Two other services also were part of the Teaching Library: the Media Resources Center (MRC) and the Library Graphics Service. Many institutions will recognize quirky reporting lines based on history or the need to put a service somewhere on an organization chart that does not always make organizational sense. The Media Research Center reported to the Teaching Library because it had reported to Moffitt Undergraduate Library. One of the staff of the MRC was a crack cataloger who cataloged films, videos and DVDs with rich access points, insuring that non-print materials were integrated into the catalog and into teaching. Streaming audio was part of the MRC Web site early on. In addition to giving instructional sessions for undergraduates and faculty seminars, the Head of MRC also taught in the film department on campus.

Having the Library Graphics Service reporting to the Teaching Library was a positive surprise that helped raise TLIB's visibility on campus. While this reporting relationship made little sense organizationally, it was a definite advantage. UC Berkeley's Graphics Service, consisting of two graphic designers, produces more beautiful, professional-looking materials than in

---

[8] From original User Research Coordinator position posting.
[9] See, for example, Maughan, P. D. "Assessing information literacy among undergraduates: a discussion of the literature and the University of California-Berkeley assessment experience." *College & Research Libraries*, v. 62 no. 1 (January 2001) p. 71-85
[10] For more information on the activities of the User Research Coordinator, see http://www.lib.berkeley.edu/userresearch/
[11] See also http://www.lib.berkeley.edu/autobiography/pmaughan/publications.html

any library I have ever visited. This office was responsible for library signage, library exhibit labels, Web design, range finder signs for the fifty-five miles of stack ranges in the Main (Doe) Library Gardner stacks, and more. Because they were part of TLIB, they were very responsive to Teaching Library requests, and they brought the point of view and creativity of artists to discussions with the entire Teaching Library team.

What contributed to the success of the Teaching Library?

There were several factors contributing to the Teaching Library's success, and many of these could be used for launching new library services still today. First was support and enthusiasm from the university library administration. Since this was a new slant for the library, and library administration felt responsible in part for this new direction, and the Teaching Library truly supported student and faculty learning, there was strong buy-in for this new service and style of creating and managing a library unit. Administrative support is a key factor to the success of any library initiatives, but especially for launching new ones.

Second, the idea of belonging to a new library unit was very appealing to the people who applied for Teaching Library positions. TLIB had a certain *élan vital* that drove its members. There was a pioneering spirit, a "we can do it!" attitude motivating the Teaching Library team. The group was very cooperative and supportive of each other's areas. There was no attitude of "Sorry, I'm too busy to do an instructional session for you." If someone needed help in planning classes or programs there was very much a spirit of,

"How can I help?" From the administrative assistant on up, the Teaching Library was a joint entity.

Furnishing a new imprint and name to a service that was in many ways similar to what we were already doing added to the Teaching Library's success. "What's the Teaching Library?" colleagues across campus would ask. With a new logo, newly recruited staff, and a new internal structure, joined with a new enthusiasm for our work, a buzz was created on campus about the Teaching Library and our services.

Brainstorming was the norm in the Teaching Library. When it came time for activities such as creating enticing posters for drop-in instructional sessions (which were largely successful), the group allowed ideas to flow freely and came up with wonderful ideas that were turned into fabulous designs by the library's graphic designer.

Another key to the success of the Teaching Library was that staff had a willingness to innovate. When library administrators asked TLIB staff if something were possible, if we could run a new service or support a class in a technologically inventive way, the staff would try to support it no matter how busy we were or how impossible the task seemed. Staff would seek out help behind the scenes, pull out their hair, but do everything to support innovation. Saying "yes" first and worrying about "how" later often helped in gaining increased support for the Teaching Library.

Another key to the success of the Teaching Library was its international visibility. During the first few years of the Teaching Library, Anne Lipow was a frequent trainer in libraries across Australia and New Zealand. She facilitated discussions and gave talks on topics such as Virtual Reference, the Library without Walls, and Reference Service in the Digital Environment. I don't know exactly what Anne ever said about the Teaching Library, but I received frequent requests to meet and discuss it to visiting librarians from around the world. These visits provided wonderful opportunities to talk and learn from visiting librarians. Moreover, through visitors, the ideas generated by the Teaching Library had wider discussion.

I left the Teaching Library in 2001, and its third Head came to the library in June, 2007. Much of the openness, willingness to innovate, team spirit, managing to the strengths of staff, and focusing on end users can find inspiration in Anne's own life and career. In whatever shape library services takes in the next decades, I hope those qualities Anne best embodied continue on.

Anne, an inspiration

An aside about Anne: Anne had a wonderful quality of inclusiveness in her enthusiasm, and I consider myself so lucky to have experienced that and to be able to carry some of her enthusiasm on. She was someone who was always light years ahead of everyone else in terms of her creativity. (In fact, when the library sponsored an ARL Creativity workshop, and the staff lined up in order of their scores after taking a creativity assessment, Anne fell at the far end of the creativity scale.) She had an incredible talent for mixing vision, humor, and absurdity that would sometimes be just on the border of total outrageousness. One example was in the early 1980's when it was clear the library world was headed in a whole new direction. The Melvyl Catalog, the union catalog of the University of California was in the works. UC Berkeley's University Librarian was Joe Rosenthal, a shy and circumspect man whose shyness could be construed as aloofness. He was someone with the smarts to know you could only accomplish two or three major initiatives during one's tenure as University Librarian. One of these was the retrospective conversion of the card catalog to electronic format. He had the will to do it, but lacked the charisma to motivate the library staff to use and train patrons to use catalogs on microfiche that were an interim outcome of recon. Not surprisingly, Anne came up with an unlikely, wacky idea: she somehow got Joe to agree (I would have liked to be in on THAT meeting!) to have small red books printed, about three by three inches in size, entitled *Quotations from Chairman Joe*. The Little Red Book, as it was referred to (taking a cue from Chairman Mao's *Little Red Book*), was distributed to everyone in the Library. Public service staff, delighted by this unlikely incentive, were able to get behind teaching people how to use the microfiche catalogs. (These truly represented one of the low points in library history.) This was a quintessential Anne project!

Virtual Reference Interviewing and Neutral Questioning

Allison A. Cowgill, Louise Feldmann, and A. Robin Bowles

While I did not know Anne Grodzins Lipow personally, I went to a program on reference interviewing and neutral questioning that she did at a Nevada Library Association conference in the late 1980s. This was one of the best sessions I have attended at any local, state, regional or national conference. I was so impressed that I still refer to Anne's handouts when I conduct reference interviewing training sessions. She was one of the first librarians to discuss using neutral questioning techniques in the virtual environment. As we know, Anne became an articulate proponent of virtual reference services; her major publications on this topic include *Establishing a Virtual Reference Service: VRS Training Manual*, co-authored with Steve Coffman (2001) and *The Virtual Reference Librarian's Handbook* (2003). Her articles on reference services, including virtual reference, appeared in periodicals such as *Library Journal, Reference & User Services Quarterly*, and *Reference Services Review*. We hope this effort honors some of Anne Lipow's many accomplishments. — Allison A. Cowgill

The Reference Interview

Librarians have "long recognized the tendency of library users to pose their initial questions in incomplete, often unclear, and sometimes covert terms."[12] Some users may be hesitant to ask questions and when they do, their questions do not necessarily convey what they want. Other patrons may not

Allison Cowgill is the Psychology, Sociology and Political Sciences librarian and Louise Feldmann is the Business and Economics Librarian at Colorado State University. Robin Bowles, formerly a temporary science librarian at Colorado State, is now at the Swedish Medical Center Library in Denver, Colorado.

Technology in Libraries: Essays in Honor of Anne Grodzins Lipow, ed. Roy Tennant. Lulu.com, 2008.

---

[12] Patricia Dewdney, "Asking 'Why' Questions in the Reference Interview: A Theoretical Justification," *Library Quarterly* 67, no. 1 (1997): 51.

have fully defined to themselves what they need or they may insist on using specific sources when librarians can readily identify alternatives that are much more helpful.

Questioning during the reference interview may elicit more information about: what the user wants to know; how the user plans to use the information; and what level of detail, technical specialization, or reading ability would be best. Questions also help the librarian to determine what format of information is preferred and identify other restrictions, about the amount of work the user is willing to do, concerns about time limits or deadlines, and or if only the most recent information will do.[13]

According to the American Library Association's Reference and User Services Association (RUSA), "the reference interview is the heart of the reference transaction and is crucial to the success of the process ... strong listening and questioning skills are necessary for a positive interaction."[14]

The librarian uses open-ended questioning techniques to encourage patrons to expand on the request or present additional information. Some examples of such questions include:

- Please tell me more about your topic.

- What additional information can you give me?

- How much information do you need?

The librarian uses closed and/or clarifying questions to refine the search query. Some examples of clarifying questions are:

- What have you already found?

- What type of information do you need (books, articles, etc.)?

---

[13] Catherine Sheldrick Ross, Kirsti Nilsen, and Patricia Dewdney, *Conducting the Reference Interview* (New York: Neal Schuman Publishers, Inc.: 2002): 4.

[14] Reference and Users Service Association, American Library Association, "Guidelines for Behavioral Performance of Reference and Information Service Providers," http://www.ala.org/ala/rusa/rusaprotools/referenceguide/guidelinesbehavioral.htm (accessed 7 July 2007).

- Do you need current or historical information?[15]

Bill Katz, the highly respected author of *Introduction to Reference Work*, states that "the reference interview points up the true nature of reference service. It is an art form with different responses for different people, different situations."[16] It involves listening, being approachable, and using verbal and nonverbal cues in order to understand what patrons want.[17]

Virtual Reference Interviewing

Discussions on virtual reference began in the late 1990s and journal articles and conferences, such as the annual Virtual Reference Desk Conferences that began in 1999, widely promoted this new service. Books soon followed. Some major monographs include: *The Virtual Reference Desk: Creating a Reference Future* edited by R. David Lankes, et.al (2004); *The Virtual Reference Experience: Integrating Theory into Practice* edited by R. David Lankes, et.al. (2004); *Virtual Reference Training: The Complete Guide to Providing Anytime Anywhere Answers* by Buff Hirko and Mary Bucher Ross (2004); and *The Virtual Reference Librarians Handbook* by Anne Grodzins Lipow (2003). Other works, such as *Reference and Information Services in the 21st Century: An Introduction* by Kay Cassell and Uma Hiremath (2006), cover virtual reference as one part of a larger discussion on library public services. Libraries of all types and sizes throughout the United States now offer Internet-based chat reference assistance.

Materials on virtual reference cover a wide range of topics including staff training, service implementation and maintenance, consortial agreements, software selection, policies and best practices, service assessment, ongoing research agendas, and concerns about its usefulness and costs. Many works discuss the importance of reference interviewing in the chat environment. In its "Guidelines for Implementing and Maintaining Virtual Reference Services," RUSA states that "standard guidelines of reference service (such as

---

[15] Ibid.

[16] Bill Katz, *Introduction to Reference Work: Reference Services and Reference Processes*, Vol. 2, 8th ed. (Boston: McGraw Hill, 2002): 125.

[17] Ibid., 134-135.

reference interviewing, exchange of questions between services, et al.) should prevail" and "staff should follow interpersonal communication practices that promote effective provision of reference service."[18] Cassell and Hiremath concur: "librarians should approach the virtual reference question in the same way as a face-to-face one" and "proceed to do a reference interview, asking the user for the context of the query, followed by open-ended questions."[19] In *Virtual Reference Training: The Complete Guide to Providing Anytime Anywhere Answers*, Buff Hirko and Mary Bucher Ross also address the importance of asking open-ended questions in online reference interviews.[20]

While traditional reference interviewing techniques are used in the virtual environment, many librarians readily agree that reference interviewing in the computer-mediated environment is quite dissimilar. In virtual reference, some patrons may expect answers relatively quickly and do not understand why they are asked so many questions. Problems with software and connectivity are decidedly frustrating for both librarians and patrons and compound the challenges of determining what is really needed. Jana Ronan, stressing that "text-based chat is very different," discusses the "lack of nonverbal cues, such as body language or gestures" and the "lack of voice intonation or accents."[21] Librarians routinely rely on these cues at reference desks, and patrons also use them when they interact with librarians who are helping them. Ronan suggests:

- using open-ended questioning techniques;
- using popular texting abbreviations with patrons who are familiar with them;
- communicating understanding and empathy;

---

[18] MARS Digital Reference Guidelines Ad Hoc Committee, Reference and User Services Association, American Library Association, "Guidelines for Implementing and Maintaining Virtual Reference Services," http://www.ala.org/ala/rusa/rusaprotools/referenceguide/virtrefguidelines.htm (accessed 7 July 2007).

[19] Kay Ann Cassell, and Uma Hiremath, *Reference and Information Services in the 21st Century: An Introduction* (New York: Neal Schuman Publishers, Inc., 2006): 24.

[20] Buff Hirko, and Mary Bucher Ross, *Virtual Reference Training: The Complete Guide to Providing Anytime Anywhere Answers* (Chicago: American Library Association, 2004): 78.

[21] Jana Ronan, "The Reference Interview Online," *Reference and User Services Quarterly* 43 (Fall 2003): 43.

- determining appropriate levels of formality and informality;
- providing updates to users while working on their questions; and
- determining if results meet patron needs.[22]

Hirko and Ross state that "Like in-person and telephone reference communications, the online interaction between the librarian and the customer is complex."[23] Participants in their VRS training sessions reported that online reference interviewing was "prone to failure" and Hirko and Ross found that "many queries were treated superficially" in practice exercises.[24] In her study of chat interactions, Ronan notes that "transcripts revealed that surprisingly few librarians and library staff took the time to clarify the goals of the user's research or to simply rephrase the question at the beginning of the transaction."[25] Using neutral questioning techniques is certainly one way to improve reference interviewing in the chat environment.

Neutral Questioning

Neutral questioning was developed to improve reference interviewing outcomes. Brenda Dervin and Patricia Dewdney define neutral questions as a subset of open questions that:

> guide the conversation along dimensions that are relevant to
> all information-seeking situations. The neutral questioning
> strategy directs the librarian to learn from the user the nature
> of the underlying situation, the gaps faced, and the expected
> uses.[26]

---

[22] Ibid., 43-44.

[23] Buff Hirko, and Mary Bucher Ross, *Virtual Reference Training: The Complete Guide to Providing Anytime, Anywhere Answers* (Chicago: American Librarian Association, 2004): 74

[24] Ibid., 74-78.

[25] Jana Ronan, "Application of Reference Guidelines in Chat Reference Interactions: A Study of Online Reference Skills," *College & Undergraduate Libraries* 13, no. 4 (2006): 15.

[26] Brenda Dervin, and Patricia Dewdney, "Neutral Questioning: A New Approach to the Reference Interview," *RQ* 25 (Summer 1986): 508-509.

More importantly perhaps, neutral questioning allows "the librarian to understand the query from the user's viewpoint. Neutral questions are open in form, avoid premature diagnosis of the problem, and structure the interview along dimensions important to users."[27] Anne Grodzins Lipow believes neutral questions leave "control of the interview in the patron's hands and assures success from the patron's point of view."[28] It is easy for librarians to quickly make incorrect assumptions about reference questions and then provide information and resources that do not meet user needs. While Dervin and Dewdney note that "closed, open, and neutral questions are all options and all appropriate under different circumstances," they stress that neutral questions help librarians overcome "assumptions based on initial statements" and "past experiences."

Neutral questions are also known as "sense-making questions" and according to Ross, Nilsen, and Dewdney, they "provide more structure than open questions, but are less likely to lead to premature diagnosis than closed questions."[29] They use the following examples to illustrate how closed, open and neutral questions, and their outcomes, differ:

User question: Excuse me, but can you tell me where to find information on travel?

> *Librarian's closed response*: Would you like a book on travel –
> a travel guide? (closed question that makes an assumption)
>
> User: Yes, I guess so. Thanks.
>
> Librarian: Our travel guides are over there [points to shelves].
>
>
> *Librarian's open response*: What sort of travel information do
> you have in mind? (encourages the user to say more)

---

[27] Ibid., 506.
[28] Anne Lipow, "Reference Workshop / Neutral Questioning," (n.d.): 1
[29] Catherine Sheldrick Ross, Kirsti Nilsen, and Patricia Dewdney, *Conducting the Reference Interview* (New York: Neal Schuman Publishers, Inc., 2002): 93.

User: Information on New York City. I'm traveling there next month.

Librarian: We have several good travel guides to New York City. Here's the *Fodor's Guide*, etc.

Librarian's sense-making/neutral question response: We have quite a lot of travel information in different parts of the library. If you could tell me how you would be using this information, I could help you find something.

User: I need New York City information. I'd like to read up on plays that will be on in New York next month so I can order some tickets in advance.

Librarian: Ok, you want to learn about what's playing in New York so you can order tickets. (acknowledgment) You'll need really current information for that, and so the Internet would be a good place to look, etc.[30]

Ross, Nilsen and Dewdney add that librarians do not usually use neutral questioning but state that "they can learn to use this skill and they can use it intentionally."[31] As the examples above illustrate, it is a valuable tool for clearly identifying what patrons want.

Some background on neutral questioning highlights how it was developed. Professor Brenda Dervin, Ohio State University School of Communication, wondered how libraries can better serve their users:

Library research needs to ask how the librarian can intervene usefully with users presenting different situation needs at

---

[30] Ibid., 94-95.
[31] Ibid., 98.

different points in time? ... What questions can he ask? How can he enter the user's informing processes? What can he deliver that will be "informing" to that unique individual?[32]

Much of Dervin's subsequent research focused on how people find and use information. She uses the term "sense-making to refer to her model of information seeking, which really deals with how people 'make sense' of the world." People "contact or come to libraries when some "gap in their understanding ... must be filled before they can achieve a goal."[33] Reference librarians, then, "need to know three things: (1) the *situation* the person is in, (2) the *gaps* in his or her understanding, and (3) the *uses* or helps – what the person would like to do as a result of bridging this gap."[34] Dervin's sense-making methodology has also been used in classrooms, information centers, counseling services, public information campaigns, and web site design.[35]

Neutral Questioning and Virtual Reference

Neutral questioning is also a valuable technique in virtual reference because incorrect assumptions about user needs are as easy, if not easier, to make online. As noted earlier, little has been written about applying it in chat reference. Interestingly, Anne Grodzins Lipow and Steve Coffman first addressed the importance of neutral questioning in chat reference in 2001. In their discussion on interviewing in *Establishing a Virtual Reference Service*, they listed sample questions that "elicit the client's goals:"

- Can you describe the kind of information you would like to find?
- Is there a specific question you are trying to answer?

---

[32] Brenda Dervin, "Useful Theory for Librarianship: Communication, Not Information," *Drexel Library Quarterly* 13, no. 3 (1977): 29.

[33] Catherine Sheldrick Ross, Kirsti Nilsen, and Patricia Dewdney, *Conducting the Reference Interview* (New York: Neal Schuman Publishers, Inc., 2002): 93.

[34] Ibid., 93-94.

[35] Brenda Dervin, "Welcome to the Sense-Making Methodology Site," http://communication.sbs.ohio-state.edu/sense-making/ (accessed 11 July 2007). This site provides a great deal of information on the topic including references to articles, papers, dissertations, theses, conferences, and workshops, and a variety of methodology applications.

- What are you hoping to find?
- Tell me what you're ultimately trying to do, so I can head in the right direction.
- Can you give me a little background on your interest in this?[36]

Lipow continues her discussion of neutral questioning in the chat environment in *The Virtual Reference Librarian's Handbook*:

> In the chat medium ... in which the question comes to you in text form, the client's words may seem less tentative, more thought out (If it's in print, believe it), so you are likely to start your fingers flying over the keyboard as soon as you see the question. Because skipping that initial interview can lead to wasting precious time, you'll be a more efficient searcher if your knee-jerk response is a neutral question rather than simply jumping immediately to answer the question as first asked.[37]

Lipow succinctly explains what neutral questions are, provides examples of them, and recommends using them to determine if search results meet user needs.[38] She suggests that librarians "provide the client with a quick tentative answer," such as a Web resource, and then "simultaneously ask a neutral question" to elicit more information from the user.[39] She also provides specific practice exercises that use neutral questioning techniques to "get at the real question."[40] One of her examples is:

---

[36] Anne Grodzins Lipow and Steve Coffman, *Establishing a Virtual Reference Services: VRS Training Manual* (El Dorado Hills, CA: Library Solutions Press, August 2001): 1-4C.2-1.4C.3.
[37] Anne Grodzins Lipow, *The Virtual Reference Librarian's Handbook* (Berkeley, CA: Library Solutions Press; New York: Neal-Schuman Publishers, Inc., 2003): 65.
[38] Ibid., 157-160.
[39] Ibid., 159.
[40] Ibid., 68.

Client: I am looking for a copy of the Van Gogh painting called Girl with Ruffled Hair.

Librarian: Greet client and add: There are a few ways to search for this, depending on what specifically you are looking for. Can you describe what you are hoping to find?

Client: I am a painter myself and I want to paint this Van Gogh as a present for my daughter who looks just like the girl in the painting, messy hair and all! I want to make the painting in the original dimensions, but the copy I have shows the dimensions in centimeters. I was hoping the copy you found for me would give me the dimensions in inches.

Librarian: Oh, so if you give me the dimensions in centimeters and I get them converted to inches, will that fill the bill? Or will you still need the copy of the painting?

Client: Oh no, I don't need the painting itself, just the dimensions in a form I can understand. My copy gives the measurements as 35.5 cm. x 24.5 cm.

Librarian: Now that you know the real question, look for a site that converts centimeters to inches.[41]

Reference interviewing in both face-to-face and virtual encounters can be challenging even for experienced librarians. Users, needs, and situations are always different and it is easy for librarians to make incorrect assumptions about what people want. As Bill Katz notes, it really is an art. The lack of visual and auditory cues, and computer-mediated communication add to the complexity of virtual reference interviewing. Neutral questioning techniques are a valuable tool in both environments because they help librarians understand what patrons really want. As Kathleen Kern states: "we need to remember that the type and quality of the service we offer must depend on our philosophy of reference service and not on the mode of communication

---

[41] Ibid., 66.

with the user."[42] Anne Grodzins Lipow's work on neutral questioning and virtual reference interviewing is just one reflection of her articulate and profound commitment to user-focused library services. The library community – librarians and users – have all benefited from her many efforts.

---

[42] Kathleen, Kern. "Communication, Patron Satisfaction, and the Reference Interview," *Reference & User Services Quarterly* 43 (Fall 2003): 49.

Users 2.0: Technology at Your Service
Darcy Del Bosque and Kimberly Chapman

It is exciting, as practicing librarians, to find a singular voice that stands out as a strong influence on the profession. Anne Grodzins Lipow provided one such voice, inspiring us to evaluate our philosophy of patron service and helping us define our professional values. Lipow's body of work encompasses many contemporary library issues, involving myriad aspects of customer service. Lipow addressed issues including patron-friendly catalogs and reference service in both traditional face-to-face and newer virtual settings, recognized the importance of training staff as part of continuous improvement in customer service, and emphasized the power of using technology to improve delivery of library services. As trends and technologies have evolved, Lipow successfully articulated how those changes could be integrated into the traditional library organization. Her position regarding library issues, including the importance of the "human factor" in reference service, has helped us shape our patron-centered service philosophy. This has impacted the reference service we strive to provide, the issues we advocate for, and the environments in which we work.

As our careers have developed, we have collaborated on a variety of projects and had countless discussions about librarianship. Through practical experience, networking with colleagues, and reading in the professional literature, we have formed ideals of what user service should

Darcy Del Bosque is the Web Services Librarian at the University of Nevada, Las Vegas. She previously held positions as Head of Electronic Information and Reference Services at the University of Texas at San Antonio and as Reference/Government Information Librarian at Texas A&M International University. She holds an MLS from Indiana University, an MA from Ohio University, and a BA from the University of Minnesota. Kimberly Chapman is Assistant Librarian on the Science-Engineering Team at the University of Arizona Libraries, and was formerly the Reference Staff Training Coordinator at the University of Texas at San Antonio. Her research interests include reference outreach services, effective library promotion, and exploring the relationship between proactive staff training and excellent customer service. Kimberly received her MLIS from the University of Texas at Austin.

Technology in Libraries: Essays in Honor of Anne Grodzins Lipow, ed. Roy Tennant. Lulu.com, 2008.

look like. During several of our projects, the ideas expressed in Anne Lipow's work have risen to the top to fuel our discussions. Many themes that Lipow discussed are evident in the philosophy of reference that guides us today. This philosophy encompasses the belief in assisting our patrons at their point-of-need, wherever that may be: whether they are physically in the library; outside of the library in other campus facilities; or using library resources and services in the online environment. We believe, as is well expressed in Lipow's writings, in striving to remove barriers, focusing on useable interfaces (e.g. catalogs, websites) and designing approachability into everything that we do: from training library staff to provide excellent customer service in person; to designing usable websites and taking full advantage of social networking software; to being out-and-about in the community as friendly, helpful, and knowledgeable resources. Putting this philosophy into action requires both understanding and mitigating the barriers encountered by patrons.

The goal — and the challenge inherent in that goal — of replacing a library-centered philosophy with a patron-centered philosophy is discovering what barriers exist from the user's perspective, and finding solutions that fit the user's way of life, to provide unimpeded access to a library's collections and services. A library's physical location can be a primary obstacle preventing patrons from getting materials and services they need, when they need them. Lipow understood this dilemma from the patron's viewpoint, stating that "...rather than thinking of our users as remote, we should recognize that we are remote from our users"[43]. Although libraries now have electronic means, with the advent of e-books and article databases, of delivering materials to "remote" users, the concept of providing materials to patrons who could not make it to the library is not new. Bookmobiles and sending books via the postal service removed physical barriers by transporting materials directly to patrons; phone reference allowed patrons to call in and get assistance without visiting the library facility. Current methods of addressing the physical limitations of the library include delivering materials electronically to patrons. Providing digital

---

[43] Lipow, Anne G. "'In Your Face' Reference Service," *Library Journal*, 124(13) (August 1999), p. 50-52.

reference services, about which Anne Lipow wrote a great deal, allows patrons to get answers from librarians using their own computers. Initially, digital reference services included email and chat reference. Many libraries have discovered that commercially-vended software products used to interface with patrons was not convenient to patrons' online habits. As librarians realized they could reach patrons more efficiently in the virtual environments patrons were using for other activities, instant messaging (IM) has become a free alternative to commercial software. This transition echoes Lipow's desire to embrace the use of new technology, while emphasizing the need of implementing technology to serve patron needs, rather than having technology drive our interactions with patrons. Instead of encouraging the patron to go to a library space that they would not otherwise use, the use of IM puts the librarian seamlessly into the patron's space, removing barriers to access. A further evolution currently being tested by many libraries is the move to providing reference via cell phone by allowing patrons to text their questions. UC Merced has pioneered this type of service allowing them to answer questions anywhere, anytime [44].

Lipow's work resonated with our user-centered philosophy as we participated in developing a librarian-on-location service, another example of removing barriers between patrons and the library. Campus wireless networks made it possible for students to access library resources from their laptops anywhere on campus; the wireless networks also made it possible for librarians to leave the library building. Librarians became "mobile," visiting various campus locations to meet students on their own turf. Reference service provision and library outreach are intertwined in this setting, increasing approachability and convenience for patrons. Lipow noted the transition to providing service to patrons in their own spaces saying, "In the physical library, the most exciting reorganization of reference service is being done by those in academic libraries who have moved their offices out of the

---

[44] Carlson, S. "Are Reference Desks Dying Out?" *Chronicle of Higher Education*, 53(33) (7/25/2007), p. A37.

library and into their constituencies' domain."[45] Lipow adds "The numbers of these in-your-face librarians – that is, librarians who cannot be overlooked or ignored – are steadily growing." In our case, technology removed barriers between us and the populations we served, allowing our campus librarians to provide reference services at the users' point-of-need. This combination of outreach and reference promoted the visibility of the library and its resources.

As the shift to user-focused thinking is undertaken, it becomes easy to see the value of bringing library resources to the user. In addition to the importance of user-focused services, Lipow pushed us in our thinking about the future of the library. Lipow's visualizations of libraries of the future emphasized her awareness that libraries were changing and that librarians needed to embrace the new developments. She stated, "What is new in any library is the pace of change: in the last 10 or so years our occupation – the tools we use to accomplish our mission, the mission itself, and even the patrons we serve – has been changing at a rate faster than it has changed in all previous decades combined; and there is no let-up in sight."[46] True to her statement, technological forces have continued to force librarianship to look at its role in society and make decisions on the ways it will adapt.

Librarians have had different reactions to the forces that are changing the profession. Some librarians have dug themselves in, clinging to the traditions of the past and unwilling to adapt to the changing environment, trying to train patrons in using outdated systems. Other librarians have taken a wait-and-see attitude, implementing new technologies after seeing them work successfully in other libraries or industries. Another approach has been to implement everything new; jumping from one project to the next as something more cutting-edge comes along. The wide range of reactions in the profession has led to uneven services in libraries, leaving librarians unsure of what to provide, and patrons unsure of what to expect.

Change is inevitable; organizations must continually reevaluate and assess how to adapt effectively to change. However, the pace of change does

---

[45] Lipow, Anne G. "'In Your Face' Reference Service," *Library Journal*, 124(13) (August 1999), p. 50-52.

[46] Lipow, Anne G. "Training For Change: Staff Development In A New Age," *Journal of Library Administration*, 10(4) (1989), p. 87-97.

not dictate that we abandon all the foundations of our profession and just haphazardly embark on the next shiny new thing. It is important to remember the guiding principles of librarianship, moving services forward in changing environments to best meet the information needs of our patrons. Just as Lipow has inspired us to create a philosophy of user service, she has also encouraged the constant reevaluation of these underlying beliefs. She states, "In reality, of course, it isn't possible to 'continue as we have.' So how do we ensure that we move forward, and not backward? We must take stock of what it takes to meet the patrons' expectation and offer new and properly staffed services that satisfy those expectations."[47] New technologies provide exciting new possibilities and librarians must evaluate, implement, and reevaluate services to ensure the best service is being provided for patrons using appropriate technologies.

Discovering where patrons spend time can help incorporate the library into spaces where services will actually be used. If users are hanging out in Second Life or MySpace, a library presence in those spaces can help reach a group of patrons that otherwise might not use library services. Lipow leads us to search for the juncture of new and old that best meets patron needs saying, "The experts in how to stay in business in a changing world say that you need to find your niche." The niche of the library can be found by careful consideration of where we have been and where patrons need us to be in the future. If we focus on a foundation of user services, technology can be evaluated based on user needs and other core values of the organization. When technology is a good fit in those areas it can be adapted alongside other services. As we move beyond virtual reference, virtual libraries and even beyond the latest Web 2.0 initiatives, what do libraries need to focus on in relation to technology to ensure we hold onto our traditional values while moving forward? Lipow suggests that we need to think about where, "... we fit in a world that has Yahoo! and online reference services provided by commercial firms...?"[48] As change occurs we should not

---

[47] Lipow, Anne G., "The Online Catalog: Exceeding Our Grasp," *American Libraries*, 20 (1989), p. 865.
[48] Lipow, Anne G., & Schlachter, G. A. "Thinking out loud: Who Will Give Reference Service in the Digital Environment?" *Reference & User Services Quarterly*, 37(2) (1997), p. 129.

be fearful of moving forward, but not rush forward without careful consideration about the best direction for the library of the future.

Lipow's writings about the libraries of the future included discussion of how to utilize current technologies in innovative ways, or depictions of best practices for the library of the future. Describing the possible partnership of the library with researchers she stated, "This scenario requires no technological development other than extension of what is available today."[49]   Again she inspires librarians to focus on how the library can take current technology and utilize it in unique ways for the support of the patron. By adapting technology to best meet users' needs and focusing on traditional core values, the library is able to find its unique niche and distinguish itself from other providers such as Wikipedia and Yahoo! Answers. Librarians should avoid implementing technology for technologies sake; yet also avoid becoming stagnant and not moving forward. Often there can be internal and/or external pressure to implement the newest technology. However, if technology is not supporting user needs effectively, efforts to focus on other initiatives that better serve patrons are warranted. The evaluation of core values and future technologies is also helpful to organizations that are reluctant to give up previous technologies that may have outlasted their usefulness...for example, subscriptions to commercially-vended chat reference products. By investigating new technologies in relation to core values and user needs, librarians can often be spurred to take the first step in the next direction, striking a balance between the implementation of technology, and the end result of meeting users' needs via the technological tools provided.

Anne Grodzins Lipow's impact on the library profession is certainly greater than the impact on two librarians who are early in their careers — yet it is by personalizing the impact of her work on our philosophy that we can truly appreciate her contributions. Anne Grodzins Lipow's ideas remain with us, in our writing, in the service we provide to our patrons, and in our thoughts about the future of the profession. The legacy of an excellent librarian is not just in the people they meet and serve, but in the

---

[49] Lipow, Anne G., & Rosenthal, J. A. "The researcher and the library: A partnership in the near future." *Library Journal*, 111 (1986), p. 156.

ideas that inspire those who follow after. Anne Grodzins Lipow reminds us to keep our priorities straight and focus on harnessing technology to serve our users more effectively — not just because the latest technology is hip!

Libraries and Distant Users: An Evolving Relationship

Samantha Hines

"Rather than thinking of our users as remote, we should instead recognize that we are remote from our users."[50] — Anne Lipow

When I was first hired as Distance Education Coordinator at the University of Montana Library, I stumbled across Anne Lipow's statement above and found it resonated with me, so much so that I have added it to my email signature to help remind me on a daily basis why I am here. The longer I am a librarian, the more I agree with her, not just from the aspect of providing services to distant students but in my library's general activities as well. Those who use libraries are changing, and their expectations of service are changing too. It is now unheard of, for example, for a library to go without its own website, or to not offer reference assistance via email or chat. How did we learn to be less of a library-as-place and more of a library-as-service? How have we changed the way libraries work and are used? And how should we continue to bridge the gap between our users and ourselves?

It seems our original motives were simple enough. We wanted to compete with the rising tides of the Internet, 24-hour news, and patrons' ability to access information anytime and anywhere. Naturally, we wanted to demonstrate and prove our relevance in this new arena. Between 1990 and 2000, Internet access in public and academic libraries went from almost non-

Samantha Schmehl Hines received her library degree from University of Illinois at Urbana-Champaign in 2003 and has worked at the University of Montana Mansfield Library in Missoula since 2004 as the Distance Education Coordinator and Social Sciences Librarian. Anne Lipow's writings on virtual reference and serving remote populations have been an inspiration to her in her current position, and inform her research and projects constantly.

Technology in Libraries: Essays in Honor of Anne Grodzins Lipow, ed. Roy Tennant. Lulu.com, 2008.

---

[50] Lipow, Anne G. "'In Your Face' Reference Service," *Library Journal* 124(13) (August 1999), p. 51.

existent to nearly omnipresent. Libraries and librarians were quite often the groundbreakers in providing Internet access to their users, and our use of technology to digitize our library catalogs, provide access electronically to resources, and communicate online via listservs and email was definitely forward-thinking.

Internet access and electronic services offered by U.S. academic libraries began to be tracked in the annual *Digest of Educational Statistics* in 1996.[51] 80.9% of institutions offered Internet access at this time. By 1998, 94.6% of academic libraries offered access.[52] Public libraries offered Internet access in 87.8% of their locations in 1998, which was up to 95.7% by 2000.[53] 35% of public schools in 1994 offered access to the Internet, versus 99% by 2002.[54]

Home and workplace access followed a similar pattern but the raw numbers of those with access lagged behind. In 1997, 16% of people in the U.S. had access to the web from home, and 14% had access from work.[55] By 2003, 54.6% of U.S. households had access to the Internet at home.[56] There still exists a significant gap, called the digital divide, between those with ready personal access to the Internet and computing technology and those who don't.

Libraries positioned themselves during this time and through to the present day to help reduce the digital divide — we get our users onto the information superhighway. Access to a computer at home varies widely based on race and income, and many public libraries see it as part of their mission to

---

[51] College and University Libraries — Summary: 1982-1996. No. 323. *Statistical Abstract of the United States: 2000 (120th Edition)*. Washington, DC: U.S. Census Bureau, 2000.

[52] Academic libraries—summary: 1998. No. 1152. *Statistical Abstract of the United States: 2003 (123rd Edition)*. Washington, DC: U.S. Census Bureau, 2003.

[53] Public library use of the Internet: 2000. No. 1155. *Statistical Abstract of the United States: 2001 (121st Edition)*. Washington, DC: U.S. Census Bureau, 2001.

[54] Public schools and instructional rooms with access to the Internet, by selected school characteristics: 1994 to 2002. No. 421. *Digest of Educational Statistics 2003*. Washington, DC: National Center for Education Statistics, 2003.

[55] Public's access to computers from work and home, by selected characteristics: 1995, 1997 and 1999. No. 8-31. *Science and Engineering Indicators, 2000*. Washington, DC: National Science Foundation, 2000.

[56] Households with computers and Internet access: 1998 and 2003. No. 1150. *Statistical Abstract of the United States: 2006 (126th Edition)*. Washington, DC: U.S. Census Bureau, 2006.

provide Internet and computer access to those who don't have it.[57]   In fact, some libraries see most of their physical users, and incidentally many of their problem patrons, in those who come to the library specifically to use the Internet.[58]

However noble and useful these intentions are, what about reaching those who are able to be online all the time, the patrons who are wired but remote from the library? As far back as 1986 librarians were imagining the library's role in a future where research could be done in an office relying upon database access and email rather than looking through the physical holdings of the library collection.[59] Key to this vision of the future was "convenient, focused interaction with the library (p. 156)," including consultations with librarians and other staff during the research process. The researcher was not left alone but was able to find most of what she needed on her own, with the library providing valuable advice and assistance over email and phone when necessary.

The ease of use, availability and speed of the Internet caused our users to expect more from the library, especially as many libraries began using and offering these new online tools as well. We were cautioned that "[u]nless we take action to close the gap between our patrons' expectations and our ability to perform, I predict we will try to serve an ever larger and more demanding user population without having the necessary resources...We must take stock of what it takes to meet the patrons' expectations and offer new and properly staffed services that satisfy those expectations".[60]

Taking stock of patron expectations was a driving force behind the movement to 'rethink' or 'reinvent reference' in the 1990s. Online services like About.com, featuring personal guides and a human touch, were seen as

---

[57] Bertot, Juan C., Charles R. McClure, P.T. Jaeger, and J. Ryan. *Public Libraries and the Internet 2006: Study Results and Findings.* Tallahassee, Fla.: Information Use Management and Policy Institute, College of Information, Florida State University, 2006.

[58] Lipow, Anne G. *The Virtual Reference Librarian's Handbook.* New York: Neal-Schuman, 2003, p. 4.

[59] Lipow, Anne G. and Joseph A. Rosenthal, "The Researcher and the Library: A Partnership In the Near Future," *Library Journal* 111 (September 1986): 154-156.

[60] Lipow, Anne G. "The Online Catalog: Exceeding Our Grasp," *American Libraries* 20 (October 1989), p. 865.

proof that those who were venturing online would still want and need help finding information. The difference was that users of the Internet were able to find these services conveniently online, rather than having to visit the reference desk during the hours the library was open. Anne Lipow stated that under these new conditions, "Library reference service will thrive only if it is as convenient to the remote user as a search engine; only if it is impossible to ignore — so 'in your face' — that to not use the service is an active choice".[61]

One of the most pioneering ways that libraries and librarians attempted to meet with remote users was through virtual reference services. Chat and email reference, often in consortia with other libraries to ensure 24/7 coverage, began to be offered more and more widely. Asking and answering questions became less associated with the reference desk and more a service that libraries provided in many different ways.

Dovetailing with this new service came remote access to resources. Instead of being tied to print indexes or CD-ROMs, research tools became increasingly available online to researchers outside the library and accessible at any time. More recent innovations have included distance education offerings for training and continuing education of librarians as well as for instructing our users in resources and services. Libraries also are beginning to offer access to e-books, downloadable audio books, wi-fi, and a host of other services to attract technologically savvy users.

Libraries and librarians were always meant to provide assistance to information seekers at their point of need. However, over the last thirty years, this point of need has shifted from the physical library building to the digital realm. Unfortunately, librarians are used to being somewhat invisible to our users, and this has persisted into the online sphere. We have managed to increase the convenience of our services, but not the 'in your face' attitude Anne Lipow deemed necessary. Further, Bonnie Nardi's studies on intelligent agents led her to conclude that no one besides ourselves understands exactly what we do, but that what we do, which she called 'information therapy,' is key to helping users navigate through computerized searching. She also likens librarians to a 'keystone species' — serving as protectors of diversity in the information community. Without our

---

[61] Lipow, Anne G. "'In Your Face' Reference Service," *Library Journal* 124(13) (August 1999), p. 52.

protection of the diversity of resources and defense of the human side of information, libraries may not survive.[62]

The library continues to directly compete with other, more commercial, services. Anne Lipow observed that question answering services were popping up on the web around the late 1990s and felt that these were inferior to what libraries could and did offer.[63] This has only proliferated in recent years. Some examples include Yahoo Answers, Google Answers, and AskMeNow. Questions are sent to these services, which then are answered by any interested party regardless of expertise (Yahoo Answers) or for profit (Google Answers, AskMeNow). Why would people ask unqualified strangers or pay for answers, when they could ask a trained librarian with access to a wealth of resources? Convenience is of course vital, but perhaps a key aspect to being 'in your face' is clarifying our role to users.

In 2005, OCLC produced a report on a study of the public's perception of libraries. A surprising 96% of those surveyed had visited their public library at some point, and over 60% of those surveyed were familiar with search engines on the Internet. Unfortunately, few people knew that their library had an online presence beyond a website and perhaps an online catalog. The report indicated that in the library, our brand is 'books.' That is still what our users think of first when they think of libraries, and they are still tied to the idea of library as a physical place. Search engines are the first choice for 80% of respondents when looking for information, versus 11% who turn to their library. [64]

This study demonstrates a clear and continuing need for libraries and librarians to be proactive in reaching users. If libraries continue to be associated with just 'books,' we do not stand a chance in either bridging the digital divide, since users will not think of the library as a place to access technology, or between us and our more wired users, since users will not

---

[62] Nardi, Bonnie A. "Information Ecologies: Highlights of the Keynote Address," *Reference and User Services Quarterly* 38(1) (1998): 49-50.

[63] Lipow, Anne G. "'In Your Face' Reference Service," *Library Journal* 124(13) (August 1999): 50-52.

[64] Perceptions of Libraries and Information Resources: A Report to the OCLC Membership. Dublin, Ohio: OCLC Online Computer Library Center, Inc., 2005.

think of the library as a place to use technological resources. This also raises issues regarding the role of librarians within their library and the redefinition of professional work within libraries. If librarians are no longer staffing a physical reference desk as one of their primary responsibilities, who will be? Or will the desk cease to exist? If libraries are about more than books, what defines a library?

We will continue to work at an increasing distance from our users. Some library users will always be on the cutting edge of technology, pushing us to expand the limits of our services. Other library users will need assistance moving into the newer ways of doing things as they develop. We need to 'mind the gap' between these users, and the gap between ourselves and our patrons, to become and continue to be relevant. There will likely always be a library, both physically and as a service, but only if we continually reinvent ourselves to fit in with our patrons and offer our services conveniently and ubiquitously. In order to preserve our place in the information ecology, we have to make our role more obvious in order to defend our position and that of libraries. Perhaps most importantly, we must inform our users that we provide "...relevant, quality information at no charge. No other profession is so tied to the principles of democracy; we have a code of work principles that guarantees open, equitable access; we are thought of as a lifelong learning center; we provide a range of viewpoints for our users to make informed choices. And best of all, we offer a world of information that began before the World Wide Web".[65]

---

[65] Lipow, Anne G. and Gail A. Schlachter, "Thinking Out Loud: Who Will Give Reference Service in the Digital Environment?" *Reference & User Services Quarterly* 37:2 (1997), p. 129.

Is My Library Going Down the YouTube?
Reflections on the Information Landscape
Diane Kresh

The late Anne G. Lipow would have loved YouTube. Talk about "in your face reference." She would have loved its brashness, its rawness, cheered its role as an equal opportunity employer for the inane, the bizarre, and the just plain funny. Anne died too soon. She missed out on blogs and blackberries, MySpace and Facebook, podcasts and peer-to peer, wikis and widgets. She would have been all over all of it and she would have exhorted others to give these innovations a try. I can't claim to be one of Anne's closest friends or colleagues but I can claim to have been influenced by her more than anyone else in a career that has lasted more than 30 years. Without her prodding, I might never have ventured beyond the walls of the Library of Congress. I was affected more than she knew by her generosity of spirit, her indomitability, her willingness to poke at sacred cows. Anne was a passionate person ... passionate about her work, her family, her belief in social activism, her political convictions. She believed that librarians made a difference and set

Diane Kresh is the Director of the Arlington County Virginia Public Library system. Previously, she was employed by the Library of Congress for 31 years where she oversaw a range of in-person and web-based reference and information services, including the Collaborative Digital Reference Service (now QuestionPoint), the first global, web-based, reference service. She is a frequent speaker at professional conferences and the author of several articles on digital reference services and is the editor of "The Whole Digital Library Handbook" (ALA: Chicago, IL 2007). Ms Kresh is the recipient of the 2001 Federal 100 for her role in launching the Collaborative Digital Reference Service. The award is given by Federal Computer Week to top executives from government, industry and academia who have had the greatest impact on the government systems community and who have made a difference in the way organizations develop, acquire and manage information technology. In 2003, she received the "Director's Award" from the Virtual Reference Desk for her role in creating CDRS; and in 2002, was the recipient of the Distinguished Alumnus Award from the Library School of the Catholic University for her contribution to the field of library and information science. Finally, she is the mother of two Millennials, Matthew and Nathaniel.

Technology in Libraries: Essays in Honor of Anne Grodzins Lipow, ed. Roy Tennant. Lulu.com, 2008.

out to prove, by example, how it was done. A rare combination of thinker and doer ... she had an uncanny knack for sniffing out what was in the wind and then being right there in the vanguard, ready to lead the pack in new directions. But I am getting ahead of myself.

I cannot remember a time when libraries were not a part of my life. I remember going with my mother to the Westover Branch of the Arlington County Virginia Public Library, housed in an apartment building, to get my first library card. The card was a square piece of cardstock-like material bearing a rectangular aluminum plate. I was 7 years old and able to write my own name, the legal requirement for obtaining a card. The year was 1961; the year Anne began her career at Berkeley's Library, the Iron Age before 8 track tapes, Pac-Man, the World Wide Web, the Patriot Act. The Freedom Rides to register African-Americans to vote in the South would begin that summer; Martin Luther King's "I Have a Dream Speech" was two years off. That simple card with the odd metal plate became my key card to the world. Fast forward to my first library job, an entry level position at the Library of Congress ("a summer job" between my sophomore and junior year at a local university), followed by a succession of jobs at the Nation's Library that ultimately led me to "rethink reference," to Anne herself, and then, finally, to founding the Collaborative Digital Reference Service (CDRS), now QuestionPoint. But I'm getting head of myself, again.

It was 1997 and I was in search of an oracle. The world was changing. So, too was librarianship and, more specifically, the role of reference in the library. The explosion of information and the popularity of the Internet and commercial search engines surfaced new demands and expectations. Patrons could contact librarians from anywhere, (and they did) and librarians were asked to serve increasingly diverse communities with diverse language skills and special needs. Even being a library professional was different. Where once we would have talked to one another at conferences, sat on committees or task forces, now we engaged in "group gropes" on listservs, querying, discussing, flaming, debating everything from what new software product to use, to defining new rules of email etiquette. Was reference librarianship high tech or high touch or were we headed for high noon? We needed a Sherpa, and fast. Linda Arret, then my colleague at LC, put me in touch with Anne and her consultant company Library Solutions. The short version is that through a series of workshops, open meetings and a symposium (*Reference in a Digital Age*, June 1998), an image of the future and a roadmap for how to get there began to come into view. And we discovered that we librarians had it all wrong. It wasn't the library users who were remote; rather, the library was remote from its users. In resolving to bridge the gap, we sought solutions that coalesced around three fundamental principles: to create services both to meet demand and revitalize the profession; to take the reference desk to cyberspace; and to satisfy patron requests at point of need. In 2000, with a lot of help from friends, CDRS was born.

To understand the impact of CDRS one must understand the context from which it sprang. It was the early days of technology adoption for information services. Google was not yet God but there were many other online services (remember Ask Jeeves?) vying for the attention of information consumers. Anyone with an online shingle and a clever slogan could become a self-styled expert. What was new and different about CDRS was that it combined techie innovations with the subject, standards-based, content organization and customer service strengths of information professionals and sought to operate on a global platform. After all, with Internet connectivity, any one in the world was now only a click a way. Within a couple of years, it suddenly wasn't too hard to imagine a reference service where a patron in a public library in the United Kingdom could query an online system and get reference help from a librarian at a public library in southern California ... all within a matter if hours. But more on that in a minute. CDRS combined the power of local collections and staff strengths with the diversity, availability and openness of libraries and librarians around the world, 24/7. As envisioned, the service provided several benefits to users of libraries among them: reliable and authoritative navigation services available to anyone with an Internet connection; skilled staff available to search the collections of participant institutions; extended reference desk coverage achieved through coops like 24/7 Reference; and increased visibility and support for libraries.

CDRS began with a pilot of 16 libraries ... all responding to cold calls from me and many of them leads from Anne. From the beginning, libraries of all types — special, academic, public and national — were invited to help shape and define the service. The strength of the product came from the diversity of the contributions. Each library brought its own special experience, knowledge of user behavior and needs, and subject expertise to bear on the project.

The project was built in real time, through trial and error, chunked into phases to test technical solutions and business rules defined by the participant libraries. Implementation consisted of a series of pilot tests and modifications to processes were based on results of the pilots. As we tested the solutions and added libraries, we simultaneously examined staff training needs, addressed governance by establishing a voluntary advisory board and created a funding structure to ensure the broadest participation among types of libraries and to ensure that no one library or group of libraries had to bear all of the costs of establishing and sustaining the enterprise.

The first "live" question was posed on June 29, 2000. The inquiry — regarding ancient Byzantine cuisine — was sent by EARL Ask-A-Librarian, a participating public library consortium in the UK. The request, received by the CDRS server at the Library of Congress in Washington, was matched based on subject matter, depth of detail, and time of day, and routed to the Santa Monica Public Library at 10:40 a.m. Several hours later, a list of five books was on its way to London. So the "test" worked and we were on our way. During its first month of "live" testing, the member institutions exchanged more than 300 questions, creating a virtual reference desk spanning three continents and 15 time zones.

Further pilots tested scaling, creating manual and automated back-up systems such as an "on call librarian," and built a "knowledge base" of fully searchable answered queries. As we expanded globally and added services in languages other then English, we considered cultural and political sensitivities and e-commerce and trade agreements that may affect pricing models. We performed a number of behind the scenes analyses to ensure economic sustainability, such as creating a marketing plan to attract new customers and determining the most cost-effective means of administering the network. And we continually examined the technical solutions to ensure that we had the right ones to meet our mission, and that the tools we created were easy for librarians to use.

The range of questions that caromed around the service in its early days reflected both the diversity of the users and the participant libraries.

Questions like what do astronauts listen to in space, when and where electricity was first brought to California, how many highways there are in the United States, the origin of the names of the seven continents, the costs of a loaf of bread, a gallon of gas, a house and a car in 1931, the history of popup books, and the definition of a "cheese head." All of these questions were thoroughly researched by the receiving library and returned to patrons with full source citations.

Part social network, wiki, listserv, breeding ground for dissidents, CDRS helped to revitalize the profession through leveraging the expertise of information professionals. What made it most exciting and challenging for me as the originator was that CDRS was a true collaboration among the parties. Everything was on the table for discussion as we reinvented public services and built a sense of shared purpose. The rapid development of CDRS and the technical innovations tested were the result of teamwork and the resourcefulness and prescience of the early adopters. And we could see the results ... not after years of development in highly structured committees and task group but in real time ... real people getting real information needs met. It was also the first time that the Library of Congress, long a recognized world leader in standards development, cataloging and classification and the preservation of library materials stepped in front of the pack to serve the general public.

Looking back, I can see flaws in the design and recognize that much of what we envisioned, while technically possible, could not be easily accommodated in the risk-averse library culture. But it was an enormous learning opportunity for me both personally and professionally. It opened my eyes to the power a community of shared interests can bring to a task and how by sheer dint of belief in something, one can make a difference armed with little more than spit and baling wire. The short version of CDRS is that it was a project that made relevant information available faster and more effectively to meet ever more specialized demands. The longer version is that it ushered in an era of experimentation and cross-fertilization among the pre-existing silos of librarianship — tech services, IT, in-person services — unifying them around finding new ways to harness technology to serve the public good.

Anne's presence was integral to the successful development of CDRS. In addition to her role as project oracle, she was equal parts cheerleader, provocateur, and often the conscience of the enterprise, reminding us to consider the user first and always in planning service enhancements. CDRS sought to bring libraries throughout the country into strong local, online networks — redirecting patrons to their local libraries and local resources, as well as to specialized materials that would not ordinarily be available to them. Its legacy is the migration of the traditional skills of librarianship (reference interviews, controlled vocabularies and source citations, building networks and using both online and print resources) to the online environment; to meet patrons' needs, thinking globally while acting locally.

But Anne wasn't done with me yet.

In January 2006, I left the Library of Congress and a few months later became Director of the Arlington County Virginia Public Library. The card with the partial metal jacket that lined my pockets as a kid had morphed into a piece of plastic that dangled from my key ring. I knew two things when I joined Arlington Library. I knew that I wanted to remain in the public sector where I had spent my entire working life; and I knew I wanted to pursue work that made a difference. With the latter, I felt I was continuing Anne's legacy of social activism and purposeful engagement.

The first thing I did was challenge each staff member to think about what he or she wanted Arlington County libraries to be. We are drawn to the "library business" because we answer a call to serve others; so that the citizens of a community may enjoy an enriched quality of life. (Department of True Confessions: I showed an early predilection for the field when I alphabetized my childhood baseball card collection; I also memorized parts of the *World Almanac* but that's another story). Libraries provide a number of services: entertainment and education among them. So far so good. But public libraries, if not libraries in general, are at a crossroads. The change drivers that ultimately shape us — economic, geopolitical, cultural — are prompting us to consider new ways to reach our community, however that community is defined.

Google, Amazon, Yahoo! RSS Feeds, community-based websites like Digg, web based bookmarking tools like del.icio.us, and startups (upstarts?) like LibraryThing, provide services, tools and content that rival libraries in the market place. Although the reports of Dewey's death have been greatly exaggerated (see Perry Branch Library in Gilbert, Az, the nation's first Dewey-less public library), new methods and means are being tried to make libraries less, well ... library-like. A 2005 OCLC study on the perceptions of libraries found that the public views search engines and librarians equally as "trusted advisors."[66] This is a change from just a few years ago. We all know that search engines will only get better, more reliable, more content rich. Can Google Storytime be that far off? The study also suggested librarians update the brand, lose the ssshhh, grab some street cred and get in touch with our inner hip (see NYT, July 8, 2007 "A Hipper Crowd of Shushers").

So if there is more content on the web (and I am using content to mean all formats), and it is getting easier and easier to find, what will be left for libraries to do and what will libraries do to survive? And I say, the same things we have always done: preserve materials for future generations, provide free and open access to local and global resources, support life-long learning, and serve the public good. It's not the mission or purpose of libraries that has changed, but the means of providing service. It is no longer enough to say we have stuff and lots of it; we have to push it to people at their point of need. Music to Anne's ears.

Arlington Libraries has provided me with a platform to launch and test some of my deeply held beliefs about the role of libraries in society: that they are hubs of their communities, "third places", catalysts for creativity, safe havens to test one's values and beliefs, comfort zones for the free exchange of ideas and opinions. That the library is one of the departments in Arlington County government is an added bonus, an opportunity to integrate library programs and build collections in support of the services local government provide both to sustain and renew community and to promote a high quality of life. And what better place to experiment with delivering services than a socially progressive, diverse, participative, highly educated, urban village, Smart Growth exemplar like the People's Republic of Arlington?

---

[66] Perceptions of Libraries and Information Resources: A Report to the OCLC Membership. Dublin, Ohio: OCLC Online Computer Library Center, Inc., 2005.

In January 2007, the incoming Arlington County Board chair (the position changes with the calendar), launched Fresh AIRE, or Arlington Initiative to Reduce Emissions, a year-long green program. And the library's role? To help rally the citizens to do their part and to demonstrate that it is easy being green. With most events planned for April, when National Library Week and Earth Day fortuitously collide, we promoted an awareness of global warming and other critical environmental challenges through seed and tree plantings, website tips, film screenings, loans of kill-a-watt meters so citizens could measure their home energy drains, nature walks, a one-woman show on nature-writer Rachel Carson who started it all with *Silent Spring,* yoga classes, green lit book talks, and an inter-generational community art show featuring works of art crafted from recycled materials. In short, we got green.

The library took its role and its place in the community seriously and gave residents a range of information sources and vehicles to enhance their understanding of an important community priority. We maximized the community's investment by working essentially without walls – across departmental boundaries. The program was a success because we networked with other partners both inside and outside the government – we showed that we were better together than by ourselves. Such an initiative would have been dear to Anne who, in spite of my repeated attempts to dissuade her, backed the evergreen Ralph Nader in the 2000 Presidential Election. And that decision, too, was pure Anne. Ever true to her principles, voting her conscience, no matter the cost.

This summer the American Library Association met for its annual meeting in Washington, the first time since June of 1998, 20 years since the summer of love and the San Francisco Be-In, nine years since the LC-Library Solutions–sponsored "Reference in a Digital Age." ALA annual conference was when I set aside some time to visit with Anne and catch up. And this year, as I walked the exhibit hall, where, for the first time, I was hosting the Arlington Public Library booth, my thoughts inevitably turned to Anne. In years past, Anne could be found there in the hall, holding down the fort at the Library Solutions booth, wearing a "Rethinking Reference" t-shirt, exclaiming about the latest and greatest, her enthusiasm infectious.

I have been attending some part of an ALA conference since 1980, my first conference as a newly minted library professional. ALA annual was in New York that summer and I and a few dozen colleagues from the Library of Congress rode up on a Greyhound bus. To a novice, the conference was a little overwhelming ... hundreds of meetings, thousands of people, millions of ptoducts, billions of bags of stuff. Librarians really like stuff. Having no committee responsibilities gave me the freedom to pick and choose programs of interest ... so I soaked up the exhibits, stood on line for two hours to get Maurice Sendak's autograph on a poster of *Where the Wild Things Are,* and started following an issue that had been bubbling since 1975 when a group of school board members in the Island Trees District of Long Island, New York, removed several books from school libraries, claiming they were "anti-American, anti-Christian ... and just plain filthy." The books included Bernard Malamud's *The Fixer,* Eldridge Cleaver's *Soul on Ice,* and Kurt Vonnegut's *Slaughterhouse Five.*

A lawsuit was filed in 1977 and in 1982, the U.S. Supreme Court (*Board of Education, Island Trees Union Free School District v. Pico*) ruled in favor of the books (and the students, Pico *et. al.*) affirming that "students do not shed rights to freedom of speech or expression at the schoolhouse gate" and that the First Amendment right to express ideas must be supported by an implied right to receive information and ideas. In short, the Court declared that public school boards could not ban books from school libraries merely because they dislike the ideas expressed in them. I couldn't help but recall this case in view of the Supremes' recent ruling against a high school student and his 14-foot-long "Bong Hits 4 Jesus" banner, an apparent limit of student free speech.

For this ALA annual, I found myself in the roughly the same place I was in 1980, new-ish in my job . . . no committee assignments . . . nothing I really had to do except follow my bliss. And it led me to hear:

- Lois Lowry, author of the Young Adult classic, *The Giver*, poignantly illustrate how precious freedom of choice is;
- Robert F. Kennedy, Jr. vigorously warn us that the cheaters ARE prospering; and,

- Armistead Maupin (a late substitute for a campaigning Elizabeth Edwards who, in a sweet bit of irony, was in San Francisco speaking at Pride Week) warmly and touchingly lead us by example toward tolerance and acceptance.

So I went to my 27th ALA annual conference hoping to hear something new, to be dazzled by the razzle, to be wowed, to be awed. And I discovered, instead these many reminders of why I am still here . . . in this profession, still trying to understand and serve the needs of diverse communities, still trying to protect rights as necessary to a democracy as meat is to salt, and still hoping to make a difference in the lives of others.

On Tuesday afternoon, I raced to the Convention Center to hit Harper Collins before they packed to go home to claim my most prized ALA souvenir, a black and white poster announcing a forthcoming book of portraits by Richard Avedon of John and Jackie Kennedy. JFK also knew a little something about answering the call to public service.

But it was a quote shared in a LAMA-sponsored session on Leadership that pretty well summed up my ALA experience, my career to date and my memories of Anne:

Watch your thoughts; they become words
Watch your words; they become actions
Watch your actions; they become habits
Watch your habits; they become character
Watch your character; they become destiny.
— Anonymous

Is Usability the New B.I.?
John Kupersmith

"Proponents of bibliographic instruction can be likened to a revolutionary party united by conviction ..." — journal article, 1983 [67]

"I'm pretty passionate about usability and user centered design." — e-mail from a practitioner, 2003 [68]

Dramatic changes are taking place in libraries. Information tools and systems are evolving, and a new paradigm of how libraries should relate to their users is emerging. Librarians are intently studying users' perceptions and behavior, and looking for ways to improve their experience and performance. We are adopting techniques from other fields, evolving new ones, and beginning to share both methods and results. At the same time, there are conflicts within the profession about the legitimacy and credibility of these efforts.

The year is 1982, and the movement at the center of many of these developments is variously known as library instruction, user education, or bibliographic instruction (B.I.). The recommendations of a nationwide "Think Tank" [69] on the status and future of the discipline are being

John Kupersmith has taken part in both the bibliographic instruction and usability movements. He served as user education coordinator at the University of Texas at Austin General Libraries, 1981-1987, and was a columnist for the B.I. journal Research Strategies from its first issue in 1983. He is now a reference librarian at the University of California, Berkeley, where he has been a member of the Web Advisory Group since its founding, and is active in usability work. He currently maintains a website on "Library Terms That Users Understand."

Technology in Libraries: Essays in Honor of Anne Grodzins Lipow, ed. Roy Tennant. Lulu.com, 2008.

---

[67] David W. Lewis and C. Paul Vincent, "An Initial Response ...", *Journal of Academic Librarianship* 9 (1983), 4-6.

[68] E-mail from Brenda Reeb (November 12, 2003).

[69] "Think Tank Recommendations for Bibliographic Instruction," *College & Research Libraries News* 42 (December 1981), 394-98.

hotly debated, and at UC Berkeley, Anne Lipow has just become the first head of Library Instructional Services.

Anne's innovative leadership, both at UC Berkeley and through her workshops and publications, made her an inspiration to many of us who were beginning library public services careers at the time. Her own career spanned the rise of the bibliographic instruction movement, the introduction of the Internet, virtual libraries, virtual reference, and the advent of a new movement, as libraries sought to make their online presences easier to understand and use.

Two Disciplines

There are instructive parallels between the history of B.I. in the late 1970s and early 1980s, as it grew into a recognized professional discipline, and what is happening in library usability work today. The development of both these fields is marked by a high level of personal energy and commitment, an increasing number of practitioners, a growing body of literature, the advent of formal communication mechanisms, and efforts to establish a recognized body of knowledge and generally accepted standards.

However, the road to respectability is not a smooth one. The struggles of B.I. practitioners to win respect (and funding) for their activities have something to teach us about the difficulties that usability practitioners sometimes face in getting support for their activities, in convincing administrators that their findings are valid, and in having their recommendations translated into actual changes in library websites.

Usability is deliberately meant in a broad sense here. Usability is often thought of as an "assessment activity," but this represents only a part of the picture. Seen in a larger perspective, usability focuses on the user's entire experience with the online library: what users bring to it in terms of perceptions, vocabulary, and Internet conventions they may be familiar with; how they interact with it; and how this interaction can be improved. In this sense, it encompasses both assessment and web design. Further, since usability studies often reveal underlying issues with an organization's business processes, the way a library operates its services sometimes comes into question.

One might use the term "user-centered design" to encompass all of this; but in my experience, that term is often used in a rhetorical sense, sometimes meaning little more than design that involves talking about users. In contrast to this, actual usability work brings us farther from rhetoric and closer to the user, and the decisions with the greatest impact on user success are those involving specific usability issues and empirical data.

I believe it makes sense to discuss both B.I. and usability as professional disciplines, even though they are different in some ways. They both spring from the same professional impulse to bring people and information together. They both focus on the user. They both work toward empowering the user and improving his/her experience. Although the kinds of activity and staffing required are obviously different, they both involve organized activities following (one hopes) a set of standards and protocols to achieve the desired outcomes. And, as disciplines, they have both gone through predictable stages of development.

The following table does not attempt to be a comprehensive history of either discipline, but highlights some of the parallel features in their development. In both cases, we see a pattern of increasing sophistication, specialization, organization, and communication.

B.I. in the 1970s-80s	Usability, 1990s to the present
Early focus on orientation tours and tool-based instruction in the 1960s expanded with the development of course-related programs, strategy-based instruction, infor-mation competencies, and "information literacy".	Early focus on text-based online catalog interfaces in the 1980s expanded with the introduction of web-based interfaces whose design librarians could (in some cases) control or influence. A thriving usability industry in the outside world provided models, methods, and inspiration.

Mainstreaming within libraries	
Traditionally done by individual reference librarians and subject specialists as part of their job responsibilities.	Initially done somewhat informally by individuals or small groups working on specific projects, e.g., online catalog or website design.
Need for coordination grew with the advent of large-scale orientation and course-related instruction programs. Specialized positions and job descriptions evolved, initially at larger institutions, e.g., Instruction Librarian, User Education Coordinator. Sub-specialties are beginning to appear, e.g., "E-Learning Librarian".	Increasing sophistication of test methods, equipment needs, human subjects regulations, etc. led to individuals designated with this responsibility as part of a larger job description, e.g., Web Services Librarian, Web Applications Manager. The next step, initially at larger institutions, was to create dedicated positions, e.g., User Research Coordinator, Interface & User Testing Specialist, Usability and Assessment Librarian.
Instruction has been a frequent topic for groups dealing with reference and public services. The 1980s saw the growth of specialized committees and task forces, e.g., User Education Committee.	Usability is a frequent topic for groups with wider responsibilities, e.g., Web Advisory Group, Public Interfaces Committee. Some institutions are establishing dedicated committees and task forces, e.g., Usability Working Group.[70]

[70] Several days after writing this, I learned that my own institution, which already has a Web Advisory Group, is considering formation of a Usability Working Group.

Some larger institutions established dedicated units, e.g., UC Berkeley's Teaching Library founded 1993.	OCLC's Usability Lab, founded 1990 (and a shining example to libraries and online system vendors). Some larger libraries are establishing or sharing dedicated facilities, e.g., Usability Research Labs at NCSU and University of Minnesota.

Associations and conferences	
Dedicated sections within ALA: Library Instruction Round Table (LIRT) founded 1977 ACRL Bibliographic Instruction Section (BIS) founded 1977	No dedicated section yet. Usability is addressed within several ALA divisions: ACRL, LAMA, LITA, RUSA.
Conference dedicated to the topic: Annual Conference on Library Orientation for Academic Libraries (1971-)	No dedicated conference yet, partly because of the availability of Internet communication/publication technologies (see next section).

Communications and publications	
Many significant B.I. documents were composed on typewriters,	All these media are still in use (though a typewriter can be hard to find). But beginning in the early 1980s, BITNET and later Internet e-

photocopied, shared by mail, discussed at conferences, and published in print journals and books.	mail transformed the communications environment. Listservs such as PACS-L (founded 1989), Web4Lib (1994), and Usability4Lib (2003) provided increasingly specialized venues for discussion of usability issues. Blogs provide a forum for individual writers and a communications medium through comments.
Clearinghouses and information centers: Library Orientation Exchange (LOEX) founded 1971 California Clearinghouse on Library Instruction (CCLI) founded 1973	To a great extent, websites now serve this function in various ways. Examples: - Web Advisory Group, MIT Libraries, "Usability Testing" http://libstaff.mit.edu/webgroup/usability.html - Usability Working Group, University of Michigan, "Usability Studies", http://www.lib.umich.edu/usability/ - Usability Research Lab, D.H. Hill Library, North Carolina State University, "Usability Testing of Library Websites: Selected Resources" http://www.lib.ncsu.edu/usability/library-usability.html - John Kupersmith, "Library Terms That Users Understand", http://www.jkup.net/terms.html
Journal dedicated to the topic: *Research Strategies* founded 1983	No dedicated journal yet, but usability-related articles appear in a number of venues, e.g.: *Information Technology and Libraries* *College & Research Libraries* *Journal of Academic Librarianship* *Journal of Web Librarianship* *Library Hi Tech*

	OCLC Systems & Services
Major books dedicated to the topic: John Lubans, *Educating the Library User* (1974) Beverly Renford and Linnea Hendrickson, *Bibliographic Instruction: A Handbook* (1980) Anne K. Beaubien, Sharon A. Hogan, Mary W. George, *Learning the Library: Concepts and Methods for Effective Bibliographic Instruction* (1982)	Anne Morris and Hilary Dyer, *Human Aspects of Library Automation* (1998) Garlock, Kristen L., and Sherry Piontek, *Designing Web Interfaces to Library Services and Resources* (1999) Nicole Campbell, *Usability Assessment of Library-related Web Sites : Methods and Case Studies* (2001) Elaina Norlin and CM! Winters, *Usability Testing for Library Websites : A Hands-on Guide* (2002) Andew K. Pace, *Optimizing Library Web Services: A Usability Approach* (2002) Denise Troll Covey, *Usage and Usability Assessment: Library Practices and Concerns* (2002)

Two Movements

Besides the organizational features and communication structures outlined above, B.I. and usability both arouse strong feelings in their practitioners. This is not surprising, since both stem from the same desire to understand and empower the user, both involve specialized vocabulary and techniques that differentiate them from other kinds of library work, and both demand a high level of personal involvement.

In the 1970s-80s, as instruction became part of the library mainstream and instruction librarians began to self-identify as such, the term "B.I. movement" was fairly common. The first issue of the journal *Research Strategies* contained a "reflection on the reasons why a specialized journal inevitably emerges in the life cycle of any discipline or movement," pointing out that "bibliographic instruction ... has reached the point when theory must catch up to practice." [71]

While the phrase "usability movement" is generally used in non-library contexts, library usability practitioners do have many of the characteristics of a movement. Like B.I., their work demands considerable personal involvement and calls forth a similar emotional energy. Even more than with B.I., a librarian's personal commitment to usability tends to start with a bang. It is not unusual for an individual to undergo a kind of conversion experience when he/she first witnesses or participates in a user observation test. Watching students struggle with website features that librarians take for granted gives a sense of suddenly having stepped through the looking glass, changing the way one approaches the routine assumptions of library work afterwards.

Closely related to usability is the advent of "Library 2.0" as an umbrella term for technologies and designs that increase user control and participation in the virtual library, and make the library more a part of the user's online environment. As a Google or LISZEN search will confirm, "Library 2.0 movement" is a phrase in common use. Library 2.0 proponents often have a usability background and carry their concern for the user experience into a whole new set of tools and interfaces.

Challenges

One characteristic of any movement is that it meets with resistance and challenges. The controversies surrounding B.I., particularly after the movement began to gain momentum, were highly publicized. The 1981 "Think Tank" recommendations, cited above, were a rallying point for proponents of B.I., and a lightning rod for detractors who claimed B.I. was inefficient, ineffective, a marginal activity, or a ploy to gain faculty status. The *Journal of Academic Librarianship* published a symposium containing a sharp criticism and several responses.[72] An education journal stated "BI

---

[71] Sharon Hogan and Mary George, "Start-Up Thoughts," *Research Strategies* 1 (Winter 1983), 2-3.
[72] Joanne Euster, ed. "Reactions to the Think Tank Recommendations," *Journal of Academic Librarianship* 9 (1983), 4-14.

librarians are coming to define themselves as a political movement. ... The real purpose of leading all those orientation tours is to gain political clout." [73] Within library organizations, administrators did not always accept the value of B.I. in allocating resources and setting priorities, and it was often tacked onto individual and departmental responsibilities as an unfunded mandate.

Usability is not often criticized publicly in the same way; it would take considerable bravado to stand up and say one's website should be difficult to use. However, challenges of a more subtle kind do occur. Often these battles are fought along the line between ease of use and the complexity and sometimes arcane nature of the resources involved. For example, Vaughn and Callicott (2003) claimed that "Designing a library Web site strictly for ease of use may oversimplify the breadth of content included in the site, thereby compromising the instructional mission of an academic library."[74] Instruction is sometimes proposed as a way to address usability problems by teaching users the idiosyncrasies of the system; unfortunately, such proposals generally do not give details of how this can be done with limited staff and large user populations.

There can also be gaps between test results, recommendations, and implementation. While usability tests are often successful and lead to design improvements, at other times problems that surface in testing are not addressed by changes in the website. Some problems, of course, have no easy solution; there may simply be nothing, or at least nothing that is technically feasible, for testers to recommend. Many problems have their roots in vendor software that is outside the library's direct control (while being an excellent topic for feedback to vendor representatives or discussions during contract negotiations). Some problems may involve requirements imposed by a campus or consortium of which the library's site is a part.

However, other issues involve differing perceptions of the test process and the value of its output. Usability tests often follow the standard protocol that testers not be members of the design group. Thus, usability results often

---

[73] "Tin Can Think Tank," *Learning Today* 14 (Fall 1981), 39-40.
[74] Debbie Vaughn and Burton Callicott, "Broccoli Librarianship and Google-Bred Patrons, or What's Wrong with Usability Testing?", *College & Undergraduate Libraries* 10 (2003), 1-18.

have to be "sold" to people who did not witness the testing, and who may be unfamiliar with and/or skeptical about the concept.[75] Recommendations from testers are not always accepted by design groups, and recommendations from design groups are not always accepted by administrators in making decisions about website design and content.

This situation typically takes the form of disputes over which user group should have priority in design decisions. For example, there may be tension between "novice user" features intended for students vs. "expert user" features intended for librarians or faculty. Some constituencies within the library may want convenient links on the homepage to tools that others would prefer to introduce more gradually. This is the same sort of conflict embodied in the Vaughn and Callicott article cited above.

The practice of "discount usability testing" on as few as five users[76] is valuable as a way of surfacing basic issues, especially with relatively homogeneous user populations and when used in iterative testing. Being easy to perform with limited staff and low budgets, it has in a very real way made widespread usability work possible for libraries. However, it can lead to disputes about sample size and validity that would not be so likely with a survey using a statistically significant sample.[77]

Naturally, there may also be legitimate differences in the interpretation of test results. Did an undergraduate fail to find information on loan periods because the link said "Circulation" or because it was buried in a haystack of other links and text? Does an "Electronic Journals" link on the homepage inevitably sidetrack users who need to search at the article level? Careful testing, and iterative re-testing, is needed to resolve such issues.

---

[75] For an excellent summary of these issues, see Brenda Reeb, "Communicating Usability Results," in Eric Lease Morgan, ed., *Designing, Implementing, and Maintaining Digital Library Services and Collections with MyLibrary*, n.d.: http://dewey.library.nd.edu/mylibrary/manual/ch/ch13.html. Accessed May 11, 2007.
[76] "Why You Only Need to Test With 5 Users", Jakob Nielsen's Alertbox (March 19, 2000): http://www.useit.com/alertbox/20000319.html. See also "Quantitative Studies: How Many Users to Test?", Jakob Nielsen's Alertbox (June 26, 2006): http://www.useit.com/alertbox/quantitative_testing.html. Both accessed May 11, 2007.
[77] A useful tool for ensuring an adequate sample is the Sample Size Calculator offered on the Survey System website: http://www.surveysystem.com/sscalc.htm. Accessed May 11, 2007.

Building Credibility

Up through the 1970s, B.I. drew primarily on existing educational theory and training practices for concepts and methods (e.g., setting instructional objectives or using the "progressive disclosure" technique). As the discipline matured, it evolved its own set of advanced concepts such as research strategy instruction, information literacy, and standardized information competencies. Assessment became a key issue, and remains so to this day, as practitioners attempt to make their programs as effective as possible – and justify them to administrators.

Usability practitioners in libraries rightly draw on the large and growing body of published data generated in other contexts. Many of the design patterns known to work on other kinds of websites are applicable here, especially when they are common enough that most users are familiar with them. However, library usability work has begun to generate its own body of knowledge, as individuals publish their findings, some libraries establish websites to share their test practices and results, and attempts are made to pool results from multiple tests.

What do you think is the most important "next step" for usability to evolve as a recognized professional discipline in libraries? I put this question to Usability4Lib listserv subscribers, most of whom are practitioners. Here are some of their replies:

- "Making user studies public should help the usability cause by showing the library staff, administration, and the public what usability work is being done and how the library benefits from it." [78]

- "Libraries should stop treating their web sites as an 'add-on' to their mission and web librarians need to be insisting that development can't happen without usability. Put another way, if the web site was really viewed by librarians and administrators as a primary service

---

[78] E-mail from Suzanne Chapman (April 27, 2007).

point for users then usability will ... mature to a dedicated task by some personnel in the library." [79]

- "Need to hire usability professionals from the field. I think there has to be a cultural shift, particularly in academic libraries, away from a staff centric view of the Web site to a more user -centric view." [80]

- "... we need an organization-wide embracing of the concept of user-centered design. I think we've made progress in selling the value of usability testing, but are still working on educating people about the importance of a broader approach to user-centered design." [81]

- "Usability and librarianship in general need to become much more rigorous in our methodology. I see this as a major hurdle. Beyond that we need to report results in a more rigorous and consistent way. I think that there are many lessons to be learned from evidence-based practice initiatives in other professions, and evidence based librarianship is making some strides." [82]

Convergence

I believe Anne Lipow would have liked what the usability movement is becoming. In her last published work, she challenged librarians who operate virtual reference services: "How aware are you of the usability of your Website and the degree to which it encourages or discourages use of your service?" and proposed something new for reference job descriptions: "On the premise that every question asked at the desk is evidence of the library's failure to be self-evident to the client, [the librarian] analyzes point-of-need questions with the view to eliminating categories of questions [and] suggests methods to accomplish this ..." [83]

---

[79] E-mail from Douglas Goans (April 9, 2007).
[80] E-mail from Susan Rector (April 9, 2007).
[81] E-mail from Janet Evander (April 27, 2007).
[82] E-mail from Kathleen Bauer (April 11, 2007).
[83] Lipow, Anne Grodzins. "The Librarian Has Left the Building — But To Where?" *Internet Reference Services Quarterly* 8 (2003): 9-18.

As the latter quote suggests, usability should not operate in isolation from reference – or, I would suggest, from its sister discipline of instruction. The reference desk and the classroom are both excellent venues for informal usability testing and observation. This part of the practice of usability is not limited to a small cadre of formally trained testers. Widespread staff awareness and participation is part of building a culture of usability, just as it was part of building a culture of user education in the 1980s.

In fact, the disciplines of reference, instruction, and usability are converging as reference service is offered via e-mail links, webforms, and instant messaging, and as libraries develop web-based tutorials with sound, animation, and interactivity. They are likely to converge even more as library websites offer other enhanced functions such as personalization, "best bets" recommendations, federated search boxes, and toolbars. An excellent example of this trend is Ellysa Stern Cahoy's presentation at the 2007 CIC Library Conference. Cahoy, billed as a "next generation librarian," titled her talk "Interface = Instruction" and urged that "Public service librarians have to consider interface design as part of their job." [84]

The evolving discipline of usability will not replace instruction. Instead, the two increasingly operate hand in hand. Usability work benefits from teaching and reference experiences, and in turn it influences the content and methods of instruction. Graves and Ruppel (2006) found that "instruction librarians are claiming a stake in usability testing" and are being positively affected by it. In their survey, 79% of respondents reported that participating in a usability study had changed the way they did library instruction. [85]

Websites are ultimately teaching tools, even in the "Library 1.0" world of page-based designs. In this way, they are much like library buildings. Users are constantly learning something from the online spaces in which they navigate and search, whether or not we realize it. In this respect, the

---

[84] Ellysa Stern Cahoy, "Interface = Instruction", presented at the CIC Library Conference (Minneapolis, March 19-20, 2007). The quote is taken from the conference video: http://blog.lib.umn.edu/CICLib07/2007/03/next_gen_panel_video.html. The PowerPoint presentation is also available: http://www.slideshare.net/Ellysa/cic-talk/. Both accessed May 11, 2007.
[85] Stephanie Graves and Margie Ruppel, "Usability Testing and Instruction Librarians: A Perfect Pair," *Internet Reference Services Quarterly* 11 (2006), 99-116.

following words – written in 1980 and very much part of the B.I. movement – are applicable to usability work today:

> Every user receives cues from the environment; this is true whether these cues are planned or unplanned, consistent or random, helpful or confusing. Whether the environment will be an aid or an obstacle to the user depends upon the extent to which the library acts to shape its environment as an instructional tool. [86]

---

[86] John Kupersmith, "Informational Graphics and Sign Systems as Library Instruction Media," *Drexel Library Quarterly* 16 (January 1980), 54-68. Also available at: http://www.jkup.net/graphics.html. Accessed May 11, 2007.

A Tale of the Failure of the Grand Vision of Virtual Reference, BWDIK

Karen Hunt

My 14 year-old daughter chats with several friends at once using instant messaging (IM). At the same time she gets curious about how to speak Hawaiian and starts teaching herself from something she finds on the web. She has a bunch of songs on her iPod without titles and artists and she turns to Google to find the lyrics.

The first time I met Anne Lipow, that daughter was a few weeks away from being born. I was attending one of Anne's "Rethinking Reference" workshops and I had the privilege of sitting with Anne at lunch. No doubt because I was so obviously pregnant our discussion turned to her own daughter, who at that time was in library school. I met Anne several more times at conferences over the years and her warmth and insights were always inspiring.

Anne challenged us to think about reference in different ways. Instead of the student coming to our physical desk we could reach out and provide help to students wherever they were located. Many of us took up the torch and started working with software to provide virtual reference (VR). Virtual reference software offered features such as chat, co-browsing, session transfer and management tools. Today many libraries are using instant messaging to provide help, while others are still struggling with VR software

Karen Hunt has a Master of Information Science (1989) from the University of Western Ontario and her undergraduate degree (honours) in Geography from the University of Winnipeg (1986). She's currently the Acting University Librarian at University of Winnipeg. She was the Information Literacy Coordinator at the University of Winnipeg (2000 - 2006) where she helped introduce Live Help. When she first met Anne Lipow she was a reference librarian at the University of Manitoba. Karen has two children, Tristan born in 1992 and Leslie born in 1996.

Technology in Libraries: Essays in Honor of Anne Grodzins Lipow, ed. Roy Tennant. Lulu.com, 2008.

that doesn't work well and isn't familiar to our users. In other words, I think Anne had the right idea, but many libraries went down the wrong road and are only now getting to the place where our students live. Today that's IM.

Re-reading Anne's work is either inspiring all over again or depressing. Inspiring because she is such a passionate advocate for service and depressing because many of the issues she raised have not been solved. In this article I would like to chronicle the history of virtual reference at the University of Winnipeg, identifying where we made mistakes and suggesting what we can learn from them. The University of Winnipeg is a predominately undergraduate university in Canada with less than 10,000 students.

We signed up with HumanClick in 2001. HumanClick is commercial software not specifically designed for libraries. But it was easy for us to setup and use, it was cheap, and it was simple. Students clicked on the "Live Help" button on the Library web pages and databases, and a chat window opened. Library staff could send text and links to the student but we couldn't push pages and we couldn't co-browse. The service was relatively successful. For example, in March of 2002 we had over 200 chats. At the time we discussed using IM, but it wasn't as popular as it is today, we didn't want our users to have to install software, and multi-platform applications were just being developed.[87]

After using HumanClick for a year we wanted to enhance our service with a system that could offer more features such as co-browsing. We believed we could offer a better service if we had the ability to take over a student's browser and demonstrate the often arcane and complicated interfaces we have on offer. We also wanted to partner with other libraries so we could offer the services for longer hours and share costs. This was an utter failure. The software often didn't work, our users were not familiar with the experience of someone else controlling their computer, and (in hindsight) it wasn't necessary. The software was also expensive and difficult to use. Cooperating with other libraries never got off the ground mainly because many of our questions were idiosyncratic. Because of our successful

---

[87] Tyson, Jeff and Alison Cooper, "How Instant Messaging Works," http://communication.howstuffworks.com/instant-messaging.htm.

experience with HumanClick we knew it was not the concept of virtual reference that had failed, but our implementation.

Our next solution was the open source software, Rakim, developed by Rob Casson at Miami University in Ohio. Rakim worked very well for us for several years, offering chat, the ability to push pages and basic management functions. We designed a "Live Help" logo that looked like a life preserver (and somewhat like a Campino candy), put the logo all over our web pages and in as many of our databases as possible, and promoted the service by giving out "Lifesaver" lollipops. Our Live Help service using Rakim was successful, but in the last few years we've seen a drop in use. Last year we piloted Meebo (a multi-platform IM service), and as one of our student reference assistants writes: "Having worked with both Rakim and Meebo, I would recommend the library to go with Meebo . . . Meebo has much less technical problems and is more user-friendly. Especially the user can see that UWLiveHelp is typing while UWLiveHelp is typing in Meebo. This is a very important feature to both the user and the librarian."[88]

In 2003, Anne Lipow wrote a history of virtual reference from the perspective of 2020.[89] While her vision is compelling, I don't think it is viable. "The future of reference" opens with a typically provocative statement:

"If the truth be known, as a place to get help in finding information, the reference desk was never a good idea."[90]

Anne bluntly lists some of the contradictions in our physical reference desk. Contradictions that we have lived with for so long we no longer see. Perhaps because she knew her own life would soon end, she was able to see the contradictions more clearly. She optimistically writes that there is "no doubt that point-of-need library reference service will thrive. It will no longer be an afterthought but will take center stage as the user's point of human

---

[88] Rachel Zhao, http://blog.uwinnipeg.ca/virtualstaff/ .
[89] Lipow, Anne Grodzins, "The Future of Reference: Point-of-Need Reference Service: No Longer an Afterthought," *Reference Service Review*, 31(1):31-35.
[90] Ibid., p. 32.

contact with the library and world of information."[91] The article then goes on to describe a service in 2020 where you go to "mylibrary.info", when "live service is chosen, you are greeted by a staff member of your home library . . . or research library anywhere in the world", and questions are "assigned to a librarian on duty according to a computer program that distributes the load fairly."[92] From the vantage point of 2007 we will never get there, and (IMHO) even if we could it is not where we need to be. In the dangerous world of prediction I would toss the dice of technology and user preferences and shift the focus from point-of-need to point-of-use. Where are our students learning? What is the quality of the contact between librarian and student that we should be striving for? One simple step is adding an image link to a subject librarian's IM to every course in a campus's course management system (CMS). Students are often required to use a CMS and it is the quality of the contact between student and faculty (in this case substitute librarian) that leads to student success.

I think the vision in Lipow's article is too reliant on our users "going to" a library link, too much based on a large complicated network of libraries and too much focused on complicated, feature-rich software. In a footnote in the article, Anne writes:

For several years chat technology remained an option but, as software such as CUseeMe and NetMeeting became more reliable and even voice conversations were able to be captured in text, in most libraries, chat faded away. Clients who preferred writing their question used asynchronous Web forms and e-mail services.[93]

I greatly admire Anne Lipow for bravely making this prediction, but when I see my teenager using IM, I don't see it going away soon! I think if Anne were here today she would ask us, "If every student has an iPhone, what should library services look like?" It is up to us to question our assumptions, experiment and know how our users are communicating to come up with the

---

[91] Ibid., p. 34.

[92] Chickering, A.W, and Gamson, Z.F. "Seven Principles for Good Practice in Undergraduate Education," *AAHE Bulletin*, 39(7) (1987): 3-7. The first principle is "Good Practice encourages student-faculty contact".

[93] Op cit., p.35, foonote number 7.

solutions that work today. It is up to us to be as courageous as Anne was and stop doing what doesn't work and "show that:

- the MLS makes a difference;
- we have updated our definition of constitutes professional work;
- we keep up with changes in the information industry;
- we provide equivalent service to people who do not (or will not or cannot) come into the library;
- we are responsible for the design of structures and content of our information services, but we are not necessarily the ones to be the front-line providers; and
- our instructional programs are effective."[94]

Anne's work will continue!

---

[94] Op cit., p.34.

Talking Tech: Explaining Technical Topics to a Non-Technical Audience
Roy Tennant

Teaching technical topics is difficult. Teaching technical topics to those who are not technically inclined is extremely difficult. That's why I feel blessed to have learned how to do it well from a teacher as gifted as Anne Grodzins Lipow.

When Anne first persuaded me to conquer my greatest fear by speaking in front of an audience, she was the Director of Library Education for The Library of the University of California, Berkeley. It was the late 1980s, and I had just acquired my first professional position. Beginning with a short class on how to connect to the Library catalog via a modem (at the glacial speed of 300-1200 bits per second), I learned from Anne how to teach technical topics, how to create effective handouts, and how to prompt my audience for questions as if I actually expected them to ask. Eventually I was teaching all-day workshops and giving keynote addresses to conferences.

What follows is what I learned from Anne, or from others, or from my own experience, about how to effectively teach technical topics to those to whom technology is unfamiliar or even undesirable.

Roy Tennant is a Senior Program Officer for OCLC Programs and Research. He is the owner of the Web4Lib and XML4Lib electronic discussions, and the creator and editor of Current Cites, a current awareness newsletter published every month since 1990. His books include Managing the Digital Library (2004), XML in Libraries (2002), Practical HTML: A Self-Paced Tutorial (1996), and Crossing the Internet Threshold: An Instructional Handbook (1993). Roy wrote a monthly column on digital libraries for Library Journal 1997-2007 and has written numerous articles in other professional journals. In 2003, he received the American Library Association's LITA/Library Hi Tech Award for Excellence in Communication for Continuing Education.

Technology in Libraries: Essays in Honor of Anne Grodzins Lipow, ed. Roy Tennant. Lulu.com, 2008.

Know Your Audience

Knowing to whom you are speaking is of the utmost importance. But this goes double for teaching technical topics. If you assume too much about your audience or select the wrong technical level to address, the results can be disastrous. You can actually leave your audience not only just as ignorant about your topic as when you started, but also much less likely to ever attempt learning the topic again. Once burned, twice shy.

But in reality it is more nuanced than that. Typically your audience will vary widely in their technical knowledge and level of comfort with technical topics. It's your job to find the middle ground between the inevitable edge cases. You want to aim for evaluations where a few fault you for being too technical, a few for being not technical enough, and the majority stating that it was exactly what they needed. This is the "sweet spot" for any technical presentation.

Select the Appropriate Scope

Once you have a sense of your audience, this will provide guidance about what to cover and what not. Selecting the appropriate scope is essential, since it can make or break your ability to put across your topic in an effective way. Scoped too broad and your session will be too diffuse and/or too overwhelming; scoped too narrowly and you run the risk of getting bogged down in detail or boring your audience with too little of substance.

For workshops, which tend to be longer, you may also want to prepare portions that can be either added or subtracted depending on how things are going. If you find yourself spending a lot of time covering basic material, you should know what advanced topic you can cut. Similarly, if find your audience breezes through the basics, you may want to have something ready you can easily add.

Simplify

What you don't say is more important than what you do. You must fight the natural tendency to impress your audience with your thorough knowledge. Rather, it is better to use your knowledge to decide what is most important for them to know — and therefore, what is best ignored or put off until later.

This is the single best skill of a teacher or trainer — appropriate staging of complexity.

When I first began teaching the Internet, I felt it necessary to explain where the history of the Internet. It took me several years to understand that it didn't help them in the least to *use* it, and therefore was superfluous. I should have abandoned it much sooner, and used the additional time to teach something that mattered.

A good question to ask yourself about any component of your curriculum is "Will this help them do something useful?" If it won't, it's likely not worth talking about.

Summarize

Encarta defines summarize as "to make or give a shortened version of something that has been said or written, stating its main points." Your audience will in most cases not need to know every little detail, unless the technical topic you are teaching is software coding or some specific procedure. By summarizing a topic, you allow your students to only pay attention to the most important points instead of a blizzard of detail.

Cultivate the Right Attitude

Assume that the people you are teaching are not stupid. Also do not expect them to have any particular set of skills or knowledge that is a logical precursor to what you are about to teach. More importantly, you must not disdain them for their lack of interest in what interests you. Although you may know much more than they do about a certain technical topic, they most likely know more than you do about a number of other things. Be humble. Your knowledge is probably no more important than theirs – it just supports a different goal. Anne Lipow honored all of her students by respecting them as fellow human beings and giving their questions, comments, and problems her undivided attention.

Empathize

There are many qualities that made Anne Lipow such a gifted teacher, but an essential quality is that she was never far away from the people she was teaching. She knew what they were thinking, where they would stumble, and what would most puzzle them, because she had likely tread that very same ground just before. Her empathy with students came naturally, from learning her subject by weathering the same bumps and jostles as she was now expecting her students to overcome.

It can help sometimes to not be too far ahead of those you seek to teach. In my early days of teaching technology, I distinctly remember the discomfort of being only one step ahead of those I was teaching. I lived in constant fear of being unmasked as an impostor who barely knew his subject. In retrospect, being that near to my students had a silver lining – I knew in rather vivid detail what they must be thinking and experiencing as I stood before them trying to help them make sense of what they were hearing.

Admit Your Ignorance

When you are only one step ahead of your audience, it does not take too many questions before your expertise is exhausted. At this point, do not make up an answer. You do not need to prop up a façade of expertise. Rather, it is better to be honest about the limits of your knowledge if for no other reason than to make your students feel more comfortable with the idea that even your knowledge has limits.

It is far better to admit you don't know the answer, but offer to find out the answer and get back to them later. Or, if you know of a likely source for the answer, you can also provide information on where to go to get the answer. But making up the answer will only backfire when they discover that you didn't know what you were talking about.

Deliver in Multiple Modes

Some of us learn best by reading, some by attending lectures, and many of us by doing. The point is to deliver your content in a variety of ways and allow your students to focus on the mode that is the most meaningful to them.

I recall a technique John Ober (also a friend of Anne's) used when teaching the concept of Internet packet switching. After explaining the topic in typical lecture format, he then asked us all to stand up and participate in a packet switching exercise. We all represented packets, with one group of us arranged in a line to represent a "message." He then sent us off in different directions, but all headed to the same place. When we arrived in the other part of the classroom we reassembled in the appropriate order, thus "delivering" our "message". Because of this exercise, I will never forget how packet switching works.

Repeat

Repetition is an oft-used teaching technique that is perhaps even more important when teaching technical topics to those to whom technical knowledge does not come naturally. The best way to repeat content is by presenting it from a different perspective or in a different way. It can also be useful to summarize what you have covered at the end of the presentation or at logical intervals along the way.

Make Accommodations

Any good teacher will arrive prepared. But a truly excellent one will be prepared to toss out all or part of what they prepared if they are confronted with a much different situation than they expected. If your assumptions regarding your audience are drastically wrong, for example, you may need to change what you had planned to do. These situations will test your ability as a teacher and your knowledge of the subject, but staying with what you had originally planned would be worse.

Also, avoid the common error of asking questions about your audience and then forging ahead no matter what the answers are. For example, I've seen many teachers ask if the audience knows what a particular term means. We all know that no matter how many of us raise their hands, if even one person doesn't they will still explain the term to us. So skip the useless exercise and get on with it.

Provide Opportunities to Participate

In general, audience participation is a good thing and should be a part of nearly any presentation. What you're teaching is more likely to be retained when your students are actively engaged. John Ober's packet switching exercise is one example. You will need to consider what is appropriate given your situation and topic.

Roll With the Punches

Any experienced speaker has had one disaster or another visited upon them. One of my favorite disasters happened when teaching a workshop on digitizing to about twenty librarians. We had a full array of technology in the front of the room – computers, scanners, a computer projector and an overhead projector.

The problem began when the computer I was using for the presentation began acting up. I had to abandon it and fall back on the overhead transparencies I had prepared as a backup (this was when computer projection was still new and having a backup plan was still necessary). Barely skipping a beat, I slapped the overhead transparency on the projector and continued. Then all of the equipment shutdown. We had blown a fuse. Again, barely skipping a beat, I asked them to follow along on their printouts of the slides. There was no anguish or panic, we just continued however we could and laughed it off. What might have been much more damaging to the workshop was defused into a minor incident simply by not allowing it to impede our progress.

Ask for Questions Like You Really Mean It

One of the most important lessons I learned from Anne Lipow was how to ask for questions. Nearly every lecturer I have ever witnessed would say something like "Are there any questions?", pause briefly, then charge ahead. This method of asking for questions tends to prevent people from asking questions in two main ways: 1) the question is asked in such a way that the audience gets the impression that questions are not expected; and 2) not enough time is allowed for people to realize they have a question, formulate it in a way that they feel will not embarrass themselves, and finally gather the courage to raise their hand.

These problems can be overcome by first phrasing the question properly, as "What questions do you have?", which tells the audience that you *know* they have questions. Then, even more importantly, you wait. You wait long enough to make everyone uncomfortable, at which point someone will likely have formulated a question and found the courage to ask it. If not, then you will be certain that there are no questions that anyone wanted to ask.

Be Enthusiastic

I will always remember Anne's enthusiasm. You could not be around Anne for long before being caught up in her excitement and enthusiasm for whatever topic had come to her attention. She inspired you to want to know about the topic because she herself was so enthusiastic. Like a smile, enthusiasm is contagious. Don't be dishonest, but if you are interested, engaged, and enthusiastic about the topic you're teaching, let it show. Much of the time you will end up with interested, engaged, and enthusiastic students no matter what you're teaching.

Be Authentic

One of Anne's finest attributes, in my estimation, was her purity of purpose. How she presented herself was exactly who she was. She did not prevaricate, or lie, or stab you in the back. She was direct but polite. She would display enthusiasm or confusion or dismay, and you knew that was exactly how she felt. Speaking before a group of people is a privilege that you should treat as such. They deserve knowing what you think in an honest and direct manner.

Have Fun!

No one learns very much in a dull environment. By making learning fun, you are much more likely to engage your students and therefore increase their learning. Your enjoyment of the topic can also be contagious, demonstrating to your audience that the topic can indeed be interesting and fun.

Humor is an important part of learning and of life. I always try to begin any talk or workshop with a joke that is appropriate to the time and place. Jokes that are mildly denigrating to you are even better. Since you are in the position of an "expert" it can help your audience to see you as having the same human frailties that pester them.

I have had many mentors in my career, but no one has been more important than Anne. Besides many of her techniques for teaching technical topics well, I learned valuable human traits such as humility and respect for those who lack the technical skills I possess. I saw her treat everyone as she would wish to be treated, I witnessed her confessing her ignorance to a roomful of students rather than make up an answer, and I heard her kindly admonish me to ask for questions as if I expected them. I hear her still, as does anyone I teach.

Anne Grodzins Lipow Bibliography

Arranged chronologically.

University of California, Library Affirmative Action Program for Women Committee, Anne G. Lipow, Chair. *A Report on the Status of Women Employed in the Library of the University of California, Berkeley, with Recommendations for Affirmative Action.* Berkeley, CA: University of California, Berkeley, 1971.

Quotations from Chairman Joe. The Gang of 24; Catalog Instruction Group, Berkeley, CA, 1980.

Fay, James S. and Anne Grodzins Lipow. *California Campaign Contributors: 1982 Directory.* Santa Barbara, CA: Pacific Data Resources, 1982.

Lipow, Anne Grodzins. Job Training: Developing Staff Training Plans and Your Feedback Skills: Workbook. Chicago: American Library Association, 1984.

Fay, James S., Anne G. Lipow, and Stephanie W. Fay, editors. *California Almanac.* Novato, CA: Presidio Press and Pacific Data Resources, 1984 and 1985.

Lipow, Anne Grodzins. "Prestige, Appointments, and Ready Professional Attention," *The Journal of Academic Librarianship* 11 (May 1985): 70-1.

Lipow, Anne G. and Suzanne Gallup. Public Service Under Pressure: Improving the Response: A Handbook of Themes Covered in the UC Berkeley General Library Workshop, March 19, 1986. Berkeley, CA: University of California at Berkeley Library, 1986.

Lipow, Anne Grodzins, and Joseph A. Rosenthal. "The Researcher and the Library: a Partnership in the Near Future," *Library Journal* 111 (September 1, 1986): 154-6.

Lipow, Anne Grodzins, coordinating editor. *Staff Development: A Practical Guide*. Chicago: Library Administration and Management Association, American Library Association, 1988.

Lipow, Anne Grodzins. "The Online Catalog: Exceeding Our Grasp." *American Libraries* 20 (1989): 862-5.

Lipow, Anne Grodzins. "Why Training Doesn't Stick: Who is to Blame?," *Library Trends* 38 (Summer 1989): 62-72.

Lipow, Anne Grodzins. "Training For Change: Staff Development in a New Age," *Journal of Library Administration* 10(4) (1989): 87-97.

Lipow, Anne Grodzins. "Handling the Negative Effects of an Online Catalog," In *Integrated Library Catalogs*, edited by Jenifer Cargil, 61-68. London: Meckler, 1991.

Lipow, Anne Grodzins. "Teach Online Catalog Users the MARC Format? Are You Kidding?," *The Journal of Academic Librarianship* 17 (1991): 80-5.

Lipow, Anne Grodzins. "Outreach to Faculty: Why and How." In Working With Faculty in the New Electronic Library: Papers and Session Materials Presented at the Nineteenth National LOEX Library Instruction Conference, Eastern Michigan University, 7-24. Ann Arbor, Mich.: Pierian Press, 1992.

Lipow, Anne, and Deborah Carver. *Staff Development: A Practical Guide*. Chicago, IL: American Library Association, Library Administration and Management Association, 1992.

Lipow, Anne Grodzins. "A Catalog or a Reference Tool? or, MELVYL's Exquisite Search Features You Can't Know Until Someone Tells You," *Information Technology and Libraries* 11 (1992): 281-4.

Tennant, Roy, John Ober and Anne G. Lipow. *Crossing the Internet Threshold: An Instructional Handbook.* Berkeley, CA: Library Solutions Press, 1993.

Lipow, Anne Grodzins, editor. *Rethinking Reference in Academic Libraries.* Proceedings of Library Solutions Institute No. 2, 1993. Second printing with corrections. Berkeley: Library Solutions Press, 1996.

Lipow, Anne G. and Sheila D. Creth, eds. *Building Partnerships: Computing and Library Professionals.* Proceedings of Library Solutions Institute No. 3, Chicago: 1994.

Lipow, Anne Grodzins. "Rethinking Reference in Academic Libraries (Book Review)," *Research Strategies* 12 (1994): 127.

Lipow, Anne Grodzins. "Library Solutions," In: *What Else You Can Do With a Library Degree: Career Options for the 90s and Beyond.* New York: Neal-Schuman, 1997: 199-204.

Lipow, Anne Grodzins, and Gail A. Schlachter. "Thinking out loud: Who will give reference Service in the Digital Environment?" *Reference & User Services Quarterly*, 37(2), 125-129. 1997.

Lipow, Anne Grodzins. "Reference Services in a Digital Age" *Reference & User Services Quarterly* 38(1) (Fall 1998): 47-48.

Lipow, Anne Grodzins. "Serving the Remote User: Reference Service in the Digital Environment," In *Ninth Australasian Information Online & On Disc Conference and Exhibition*, Sydney, Australia, (19-21 January 1999): 106-26, <http://www.csu.edu.au/special/online99/proceedings99/200.htm/>.

Lipow, Anne Grodzins. "'In Your Face' Reference Service" *Library Journal* 124(13) (August 1999): 50-52.

Lipow, Anne G. "Web-Blocking Internet Sites: A Summary of Findings" (12 October 2000).

Lipow, Anne Grodzins. "How to Get Started: Questions to Ask," In: *Staff Development*. Chicago: American Library Association, 2001.

Lipow, Anne Grodzins. "How to Prepare for a Specific Program," In: *Staff Development*. Chicago: American Library Association, 2001.

Lipow, Anne Grodzins and Steve Coffman. *Establishing a Virtual Reference Service: VRS Training Manual*. Berkeley, CA: Library Solutions Press, 2001.

Lipow, Anne Grodzins. *The Virtual Reference Librarian's Handbook*. New York: Neal-Schuman, 2002.

Lipow, Anne Grodzins. "Point-of-Need Reference Service: No longer an Afterthought." *RUSA Forum on the Future of Reference Services.* (2002) <http://www.ala.org/rusa/forums/lipow_forum.html>.

Lipow, Anne Grodzins. "The Future of Reference: Point-of-Need Reference Service: No Longer an Afterthought," *Reference Services Review*, 31(1) (2003): 31-5.

Lipow, Anne Grodzins. "The Librarian Has Left the Building -- But To Where?" *Internet Reference Services Quarterly*, 8(1/2) (2003): 9-18.

Index

Note: Personal names and publications are only reflected in the index when mentioned in the text, not footnotes. Likewise, section authors only appear in the index when mentioned in the text. Also, references to Anne are not noted since they completely permeate the book, as well they should.

www.ingramcontent.com/pod-product-compliance
Lightning Source LLC
LaVergne TN
LVHW042137040326
832903LV00011B/287/J